CAMBRIDGE
RECONSIDERED

CAMBRIDGE RECONSIDERED

3 ½ Centuries on the Charles

S. B. Sutton

The MIT Press
Cambridge, Massachusetts, and London, England

Copyright © 1976 by
The Massachusetts Institute of Technology

All rights reserved.
No part of this book may be reproduced
in any form or by any means, electronic or mechanical,
including photocopying, recording, or by
any information storage and retrieval system,
without permission in writing from the publisher.

Prepared for publication by
the Cambridge Bicentennial Corporation

Designed by Daniel J. McCarron

Library of Congress Catalog Card Number 76-28595

ISBN 0 262 53031 7 (paperback)

Printed in the United States of America

Contents

Foreword by Robert P. Moncreiff   vii

1. Introduction: A Tale of Three Cities   1
2. The First Immigrants   9
3. Inching toward Independence   19
4. Enter the Speculators   35
5. Reluctant City   45
6. Fifty Years a City: Filling up the Spaces   55
7. Fifty Years a City: Coming of Age   75
8. Finishing Touches   87
9. New Directions   101
10. Bad News, Good News   111

    A Note on Sources   125

    Author's Acknowledgments   127

    List of Illustrations   128

    Illustration Credits   129

    Index   130

Foreword

By Robert P. Moncreiff
Chairman, Cambridge Bicentennial Corporation

In 1876, the centennial year of the Declaration of Independence, the Cambridge Ladies Centennial Committee published a slim volume entitled *The Cambridge of 1776*, in which is set forth the fictitious diary of one Dorothy Dudley describing the events in Cambridge in the early months of the Revolution. The book is a celebration of the past. There is no sense of enthusiasm for the variety which major change had already brought to the city by the last quarter of the nineteenth century. There is only nostalgia for a better age. The inscription on the title page admonishes the reader (from the Latin of Ovid) to "Pluck with quick Hand the Fruit that is passing away." The book echoes the message of the principal orator at the observance on July 3, 1875, marking the 100th anniversary of Washington's taking command of the Continental Army in Cambridge: "Never was there so much need as now of the profoundest wisdom . . . to crystallize our chaos . . . It is in looking back to a past better than the present that men say, 'There were giants in those days.'"

How different is the tone of the graceful, sensitive, and optimistic history Ms. Sutton has given us for the Bicentennial! Like the city's Bicentennial observances themselves (which have included extensive ethnic and neighborhood programs as well as commemorations and memorials), it combines a respectful care for the past with enthusiasm for the vitality of the present. That vitality is rooted in the city's diversity—in its neighborhoods and ethnic multiplicity, in town and gown. Ms. Sutton variously describes modern Cambridge as a "battlefield" and a "salad." Both descriptions are apt—and she is surely right in suggesting that the resulting energy is cherished by Cantabrigians.

It is not clear when diversity came to be regarded as a virtue in Cambridge. One senses the beginnings of an appreciation of it in the record of Cambridge's 50th year as a city in 1896. Surely the common effort of citizens from all parts of Cambridge in the great wars of this century have strengthened mutual respect, as has the growing awareness on the part of the universities that a Cambridge which is affected by their activities exists beyond the college walls. One may even suggest that the controversial Proportional Representation system of voting instituted in the 1940s has contributed by giving minorities access to the political system—and by providing a unique biennial occasion for a cross-section of Cambridge to mingle at the Longfellow School for the five days or so it takes to count the votes. Whatever its causes, the appreciation by Cantabrigians of the diversity of the city's people and institutions is a central fact at the Bicentennial. Ms. Sutton has perceptively confirmed that fact, and she has thus provided a valuable legacy for future citizens in the form of a record of how Cambridge viewed itself at an important milestone in its history.

Cambridge Reconsidered has been prepared under the sponsorship of the Cambridge Bicentennial Corporation, the city's official agency for Bicentennial activities. It fulfills the wish of the Bicentennial Corporation that its principal Bicentennial publication should be not a reference work with scholarly footnotes but an informal and engagingly illustrated history and profile, speaking of the present as well as the past and designed to reach a large and varied audience. In service of the latter objective, the Bicentennial Corporation accepted responsibility for the cost of preparing the book (except for printing and distribution) so that it could be offered by the publisher at a relatively modest price. That responsibility was met from the contributions of many generous Cambridge citizens and organizations. Their recompense, like the recompense of the members and staff of the Bicentennial Corporation, will be the justified pride they can feel in the book they have made possible.

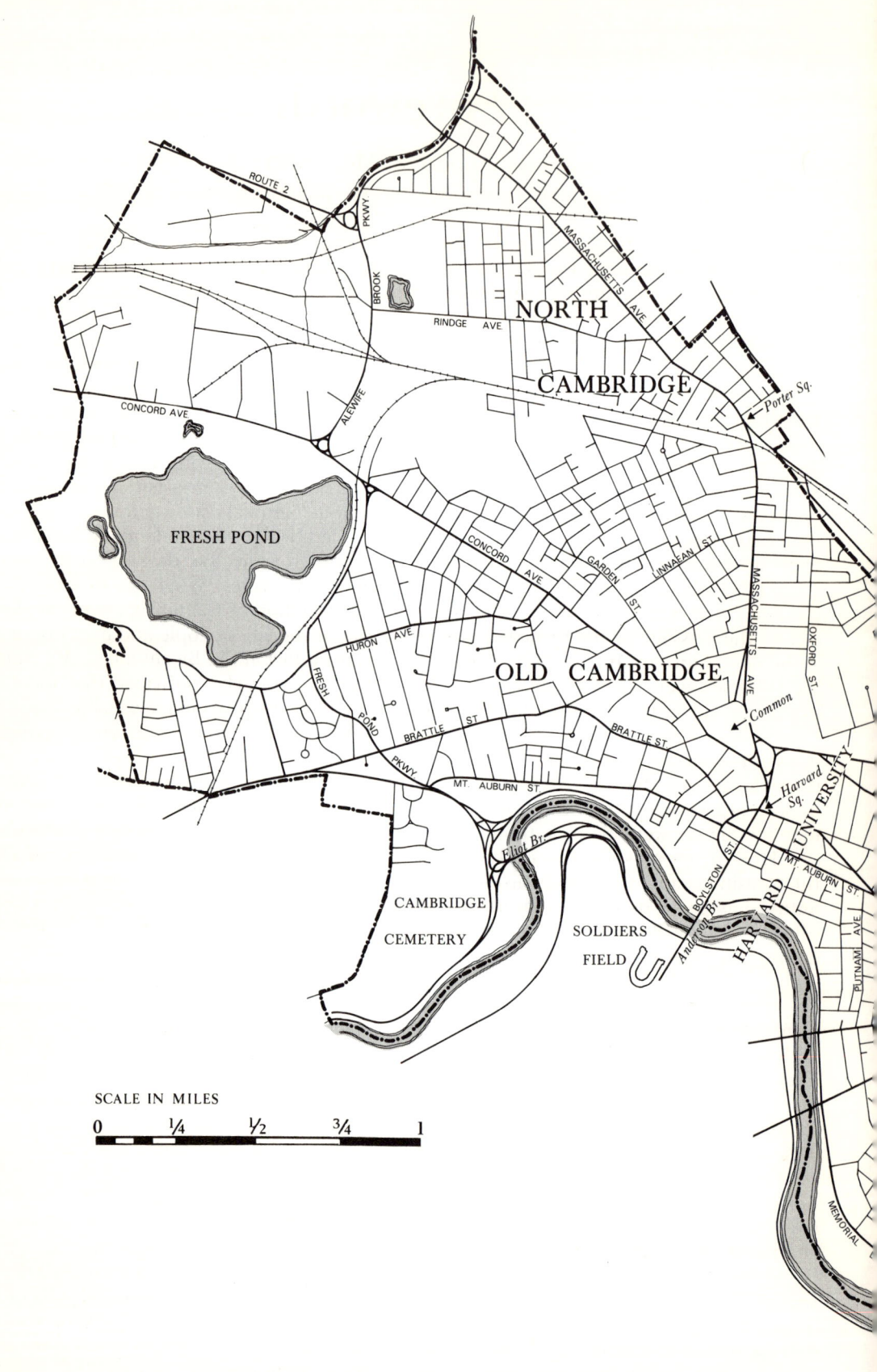

Cambridge in 1976

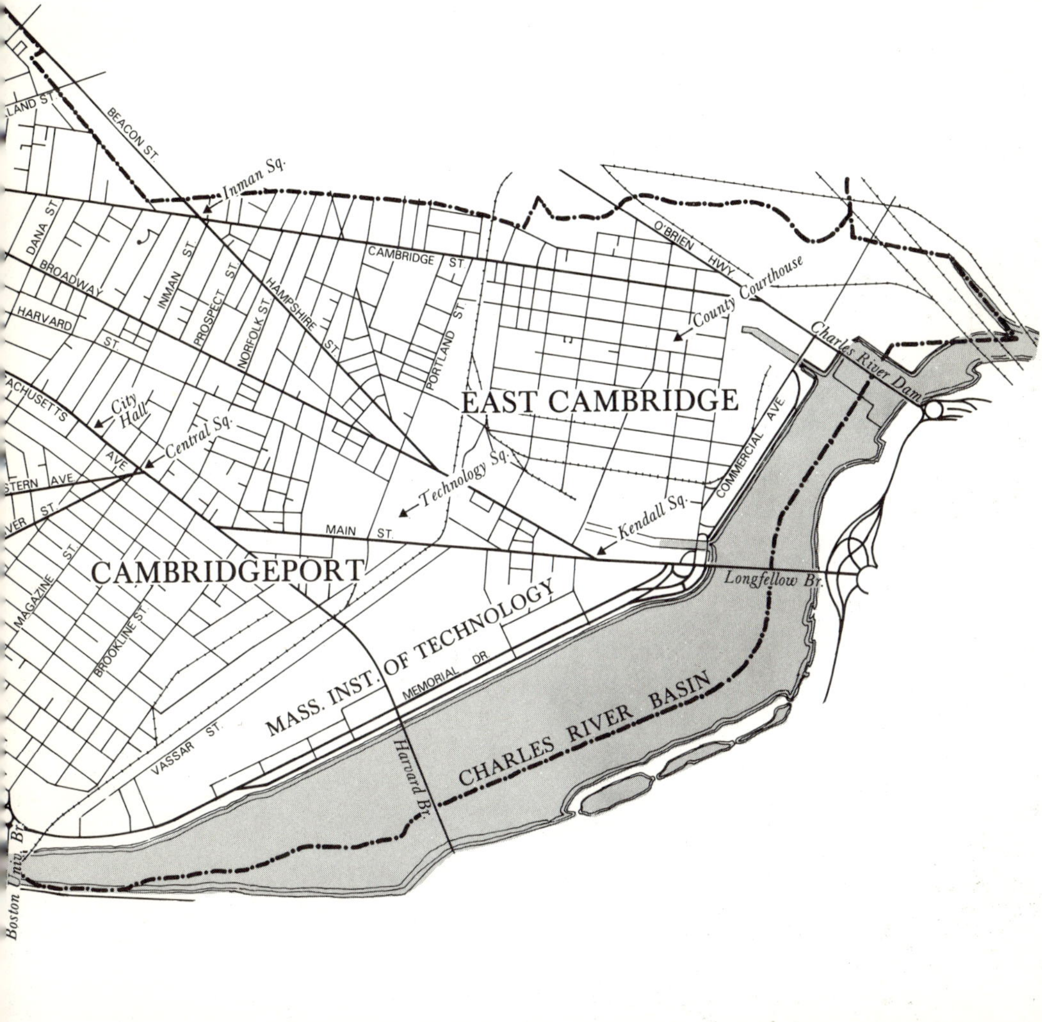

1

Introduction: A Tale of Three Cities

The way people think about Cambridge, Massachusetts, depends largely on where they live. Those who have never been there and who rely upon the press and television for their information are apt to identify the city with its two great universities, Harvard and M.I.T. There prevails among them a fuzzy image of Cambridge as a place which breeds presidential advisers and cranky critics, where there are enough Nobel Prize winners to form a baseball team with a relief pitching staff, where all the walls are covered with ivy. People who have some limited experience of the city, either as students or tourists, generally share that view, omitting the ivy. Having passed a Portuguese bakery and spied a couple of smokestacks on the horizon, they may suspect the existence of a non-academic community, but few of them discover it.

Meanwhile Cantabrigians (the word comes from *Cantabrigia,* the name the Romans gave to Cambridge, England) think of their city as a battlefield. They do not necessarily say it in so many words, but that is the impression they give. At the slightest provocation the city seems to divide itself like an amoeba into neighborhoods, income brackets, special-interest factions, or ethnic groups. The battle lines shift unpredictably. During the emotional fight over the proposed John F. Kennedy library and museum in the middle 1970s, some privileged folk who occupy gracious homes north and west of Harvard Square and who did not want the memorial built near the Square found unexpected allies in another part of the city, Cambridgeport. Residents of East Cambridge have every right to fault the historians who make little of the fact that the first house built within the present city limits was constructed by Thomas Graves in their part of town, sometime in 1629—or more than a year before building began in Old Cambridge. Then there is the perpetual rivalry between the university world and most of the people who call Cambridge home. Asked if Cambridge had ever achieved something resembling unanimity on any issue, one knowledgeable citizen furrowed her brow and replied "Yes, Beano!" Even that may not be entirely correct.

None of this is new. The town was founded by dissenters, and dissent has always had an honorable reputation in Cambridge. People have been quarreling there since 1631 when Governor John Winthrop and Deputy-Governor Thomas Dudley fell out over the building of houses. Cambridge has always been a place where strong opinions are expressed openly and with conviction. It was never a city of furtive whisperers.

For a century and a half, Cambridge grew slowly to the south of the green triangle known as the Common in the vicinity of what is now Harvard Square. Until about 1800 the community was little more than a farming village, a thoroughfare between Boston and the settlements to the northwest. Even so, Cambridge was never any ordinary small town. The presence of Harvard College rescued it from provinciality and prevented it from becoming a mere appendage of Boston.

That Harvard was the first institution of higher learning in the North American colonies is less important than that it was the *only* college from 1638, when classes began in drafty quarters, until the founding of William and Mary in Virginia in 1693. This is no trivial item. Insofar as there was an

Workmen install reflective glass in one wing of the Charles Stark Draper Laboratory near Technology Square in 1975. Steel, glass, and concrete architecture of the 1960s and 1970s has changed Cambridge's face.

CAMBRIDGE RECONSIDERED

Winslow Homer's interpretation of the exuberant activities in Harvard Yard on "Class Day." Homer's drawing appeared in *Ballou's Pictorial Drawing Room Companion,* July 3, 1858.

intellectual center in the colonies, it existed unchallenged in Cambridge during the seventeenth century. For many decades thereafter, Harvard supplied New England with teachers and ministers, thereby putting its moral and educational stamp on this new world spreading into the wilderness. Fifty-five years was a very long time in the life of a town with a short recorded history, where generations replaced one another much more rapidly than they do today. The college endowed the village with the academic flavor which still dominates the city. Then as now, people came to Cambridge to learn, to teach, or sometimes just to think, as though breathing Cambridge air would improve the quality of thought.

For more than a hundred and fifty years, the land remained largely vacant east of the present Dana Street, a few blocks from Harvard Square. Those eastern territories, however, did not escape the attention of real estate speculators who saw the advantage of their proximity to Boston. Cambridge was, and is, on the north bank of the winding Charles River, then tidal and salty. Boston was then a peninsula several miles down the river and on the other side. Though the village around the college was not exactly bursting at the seams, land in Boston was becoming scarce. Speculators had visions of population and commerce on the north bank. One bridge and a ferry had served for more than a century. Suddenly, within two decades, a pair of toll bridges leaped the river, financed by two profit-motivated corporations. The West Boston Bridge opened amidst fanfare in 1793 on the site of the current Longfellow Bridge where the subway trains come up for air. The backers had ambitious, naive plans to create a port in Cambridge—hence the designation Cambridgeport. The Canal Bridge followed in 1809, spanning the waters where the Charles River Dam now contains them and connecting Boston to Lechmere's Point. At this bridgehead East Cambridge was laid out.

It is one of history's more pleasing ironies that most of the speculators fared badly, even though their schemes ultimately succeeded in evolved forms. The Port plan proved a sensational flop, and the East Cambridge developers spent outrageous sums to make the Point attractive to settlers. But since industries and merchants eventually recognized the advantages of easy access to Boston over the bridges, the

INTRODUCTION: A TALE OF THREE CITIES

Port and the Point did not expire. When poor immigrants arrived in Boston in the mid-nineteenth century, many alighted in Cambridgeport and East Cambridge where cheap labor was in demand.

The new communities had practically nothing in common with the old village of Cambridge except a name. The three settlements remained separated for decades by expanses of farmland traversed by a few main arteries. Life in Old Cambridge revolved around the college. The Irish, Portuguese, Italians, Poles, and other immigrants who settled the Point and the Port had no interest in the esoteric activities in Harvard Yard and did not care what Longfellow said to his butcher. That academic arcadia so often depicted by authors in the nineteenth century had little meaning for deprived people fighting for jobs, food, clothing, shelter—the first elements of dignity. They hardly ever went to Harvard Square; their ties were across the bridges to Boston.

As the population swelled during the nineteenth century, streets, public transportation lines, and buildings gradually filled up the vacant lands between East Cambridge and Cambridgeport and Old Cambridge, strengthening the physical though not the spiritual ties among them. The fragments were formally incorporated into a city in 1846, over the objections of a vocal conservative element around Harvard which wanted a separate Old Cambridge. The joining was strictly contractual, rather like a pre-arranged marriage of convenience in which the partners shared little love and continued to sleep in separate bedrooms.

For Eleanor Hallowell Abbott, who grew up near Harvard in the 1870s, Old Cambridge was the *only* Cambridge.

"No view whatsoever was to be had of our humbler neighbors," she wrote in *Being Little in Cambridge*. "In a little settlement of their own . . . this little colony of jovial, industrious, yet often irascible foreigners had established themselves. From a mysterious green island far across the sea they had come, bringing many of their strange customs with them, we were given to understand.

"But for the fact that there always seemed to be more of them than there were of us, and that they invariably evinced a greater interest in washing *our* clothes or digging *our* gardens than washing or digging their own, we children personally saw little difference in them, and suffered little intrusion from them."

Walter Muir Whitehill, who attended Harvard in the 1920s and taught English to immigrants at the Cambridge YMCA at night, recalled his expeditions east of Harvard Square as forays into a social wilderness. "Central Square was as remote as Zululand; in those days the lines of demarcation were absolutely rigid." Hugh Lyons, a retired East Cambridge postman, when asked if he ever ventured into Harvard Square as a youth, looked cross and answered "What the hell would anyone go up there for?" A perceptive local newspaperman long ago described Cambridge as "an aggregation of three villages held together by visionary bonds and an absolute antagonism." The description is no longer quite appropriate. Cambridge has more than three parts now, the most notable addition being North Cambridge. The section traditionally known as Cambridgeport has fractured into smaller parts. "Absolute" is too strong a word to describe the intra-city rivalries. Nevertheless, the journalist's summary has not been obsolete for very long.

Years after Cambridgeport and East Cambridge became lively neighborhoods, nearly all writers persisted in treating Cambridge as though Harvard were the center of its universe and the remaining parts mere satellites in the college's orbit, their radiance diminishing in direct proportion to their distance from Harvard Square. When the United States celebrated its first century of independence in 1876, one writer reflected on Cambridge's past in the pages of *Harper's* monthly. The author's name did not appear with the text. Probably this was just as well, because it was not an admirable piece of prose. In an article called "Cambridge on the Charles," the author borrowed a few colonial anecdotes from more gifted historians and engaged in a half-hearted discussion of the readjustment of town boundaries up to the year

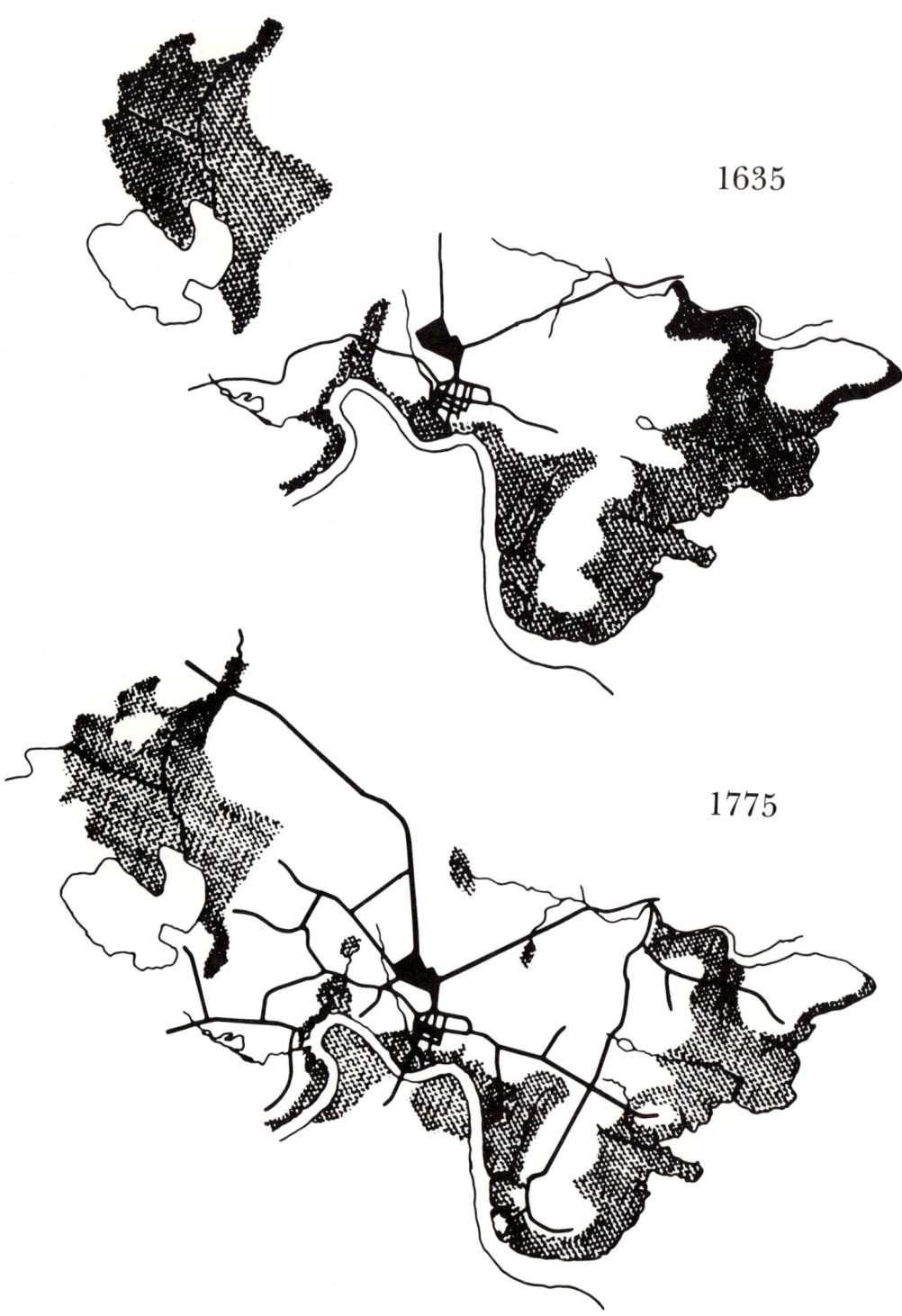

Four maps prepared by the Cambridge Historical Commission show street development of the territory that now makes up the City of Cambridge. The dates are approximate. The shaded areas represent marshes and mudflats which were eventually filled. The 1840 map clearly shows the three independently developing parts: Old Cambridge, Cambridgeport, and, at far right, rimmed by marshes, East Cambridge.

INTRODUCTION: A TALE OF THREE CITIES

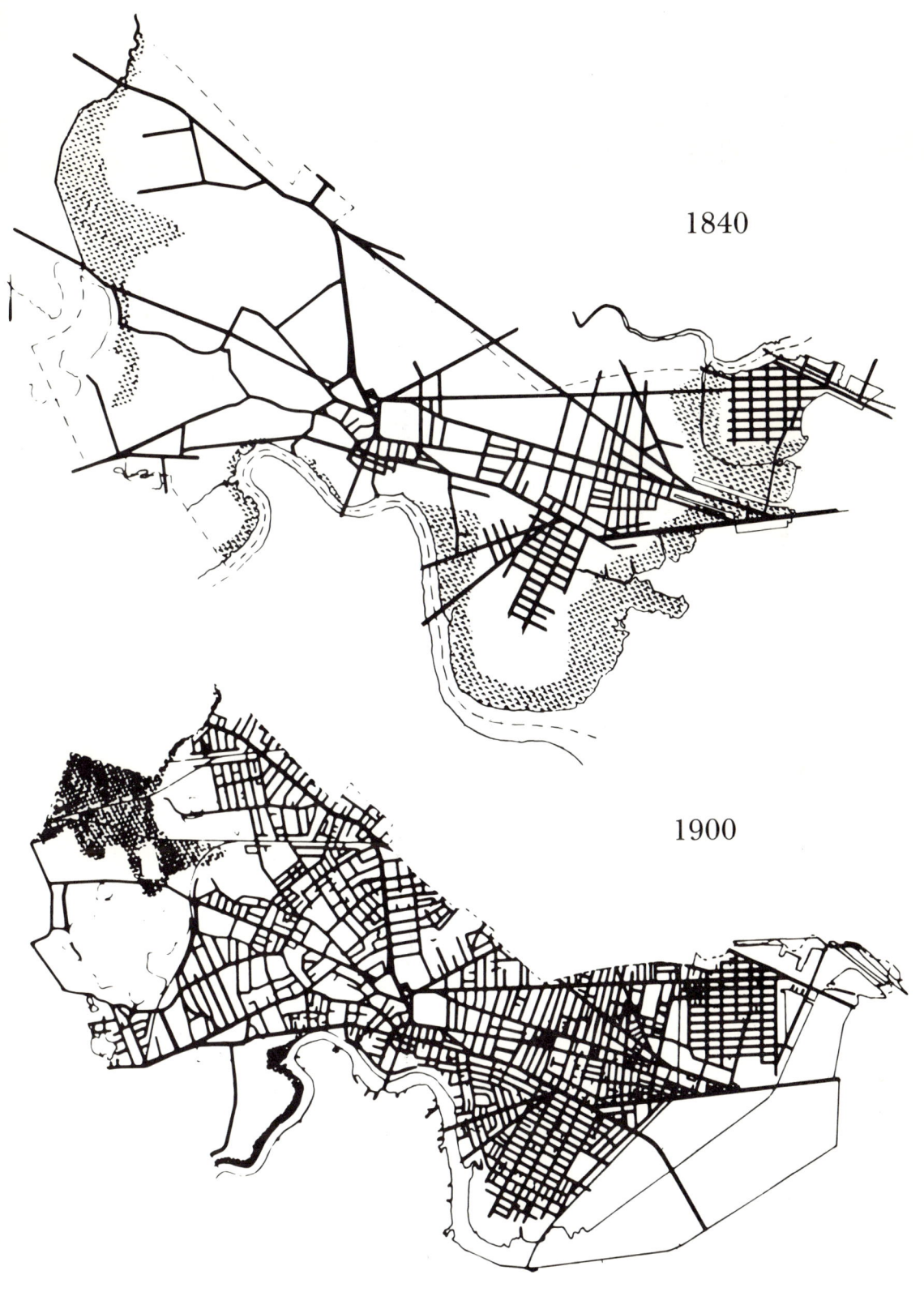

CAMBRIDGE RECONSIDERED

1732. This author, having filled two pages with such information, announced matter of factly that "the rest of the civic history of Cambridge is dull" and then condensed about a century and a half into a single sentence: "It became a city in 1846; and early in the present century its trivial commerce induced the government to make it a port of entry, whence Lechmere's Point, one of the settlements within the town limits, became Cambridgeport." With one sweep of the pen, the author had misplaced Lechmere's Point, lost East Cambridge, violated the integrity of Cambridgeport, and offended the city's not so incidental industry and commerce.

Historical inaccuracies aside, however, the author reflected the prevailing attitude of that time and the powerful grip of Harvard on Cambridge. The college long ago outgrew the two and two-thirds acres originally assigned to it and annexed real estate like an expansionist state. When the Massachusetts Institute of Technology transplanted itself from Boston to the north bank of the Charles in 1916, the academic presence in the city became even stronger. The growth of the two universities gradually forced up the prices of land and housing at the expense of Cambridge's less affluent citizens and generated a conflict which eventually became the most prominent single fact of political life in the city. Yet even those who have ample cause to complain about the impact of university expansion on their lives bear their academic adversaries a grudging respect. "There is no place like Cambridge," says John Scott, a black man from Cambridgeport. "It is homey and at the same time interesting. I even like its link with education, even if they are squeezing everybody out."

One of the strongest factors in Cambridge history lies beyond the city limits: it is the looming presence of Boston. Without Boston, Cambridge would be a college town like Princeton, New Jersey, or Hanover, New Hampshire. Harvard might still have nine million volumes and pamphlets in its libraries, but Cambridge would probably have no industry, no Greek restaurants, no subway, and no traffic jams in Harvard Square except, possibly, after football games and at Commencement.

The Old Mile Stone, long displaced from its original location in what is now Harvard Square to the adjacent Old Burying Ground, says that Boston was "8 MILES 1734 A.I." It referred to the old road through Allston, Brookline, and Roxbury. ("A.I." means Abraham Ireland, who cut the stone and who lies near it.) The eight miles on horseback have shrunk to eight minutes by subway, for during the more than three centuries of their coexistence, Boston and Cambridge have moved closer together. Originally linked only by ferry, they are now connected by seven automobile bridges, which span the river with more or less grace, as well as a foot bridge at Harvard and a street that sits on top of a dam along with the Museum of Science. Even the land masses have approached one another, both cities having added to their areas by filling the coves and marshlands in the nineteenth and twentieth centuries. Boston built the Back Bay on the south side of the Charles, greatly widening the thin neck of its peninsula. Cambridge encroached upon the river more hesitantly on the north.

Back in 1790 there had been 18,320 people in Boston, compared to the 2,115 who lived in Cambridge. Both cities reached their peaks around 1950, when Boston had 800,000 and Cambridge 120,000. Then their population statistics

Harvard Square and Harvard Yard from an airplane in the middle 1970s. You are looking approximately northeast. The hub of the Square is at lower left — the subway station on an island in the street — but the term "Harvard Square" is loosely applied to the whole commercial area spreading in three directions from that point. Adjacent to the Square and stretching across the middle of the picture is Harvard Yard, the oldest part of the university. Notice the white spire of Memorial Church, opposite to the bulky Widener Library. Beyond the spire, and outside the Yard, is Memorial Hall, cathedral-like and a century old. Flanking it, and beyond, are laboratories, museums, and other buildings, old and new, mainly devoted to the physical and social sciences.

INTRODUCTION: A TALE OF THREE CITIES

slid gently down the same curve. Both cities started with the same substantial English Puritan stock and grew in the same rhythm. When indigent immigrants arrived in Boston in the nineteenth century from foreign places where life had become intolerable for them, Cambridge caught Boston's overflow. And it has continued to act as a thoroughfare between the bigger city and outlying towns to the northwest.

Yet Cambridge never lost its identity to Boston. Edward A. Crane, Cambridge's Mayor from 1960 to 1966, used to call Boston "our biggest suburb." Cambridge has remained perversely Cambridge—in the 1970s a smallish city with barely more than 100,000 people (just slightly larger than Parma, Ohio) and a national reputation far out of proportion to its size. Those 100,000 represent most of the races, nations, religions, and opinions on the face of the earth. They cross paths frequently, because the closest thing to a ghetto in Cambridge is the intellectual community near Harvard. The city clings stubbornly to a form of choosing its officials which few people understand properly. It is a "crazy-mixed-up" place where people care deeply about the quality of life and argue passionately how to achieve it. And from the rich variety arises the vitality that makes Cambridge one of the most fascinating cities in the United States.

This is what caused Peter Manetas, a Greek-American who grew up near Central Square, to confess his love for this not always beautiful city: "I enjoy seeing someone have the guts to behave in a different way from what people who are overly conforming think is moral or proper. This differentness is one of the most enjoyable aspects of Cambridge. People come here from all over the country and from all over the world. There is nothing like it. I can just as well bump into a socialite as a Sheik from India."

2

The First Immigrants

Cambridge lies in the hill-rimmed Boston Basin. During the Ice Age, Cambridge's land assumed the approximate configurations in which the first settlers found it. The glaciers carried off topsoil and deposited in exchange a mixture of sand, clay, and stones, leaving the area—and the New England coast in general—with some of the most stubborn and frustrating agricultural terrain in North America. Fresh Pond, at the northwestern end of the city, was born when ice melted in a hollow. The Charles diminished from a mighty current of earlier ages to a small, lazy river which wandered out to sea at low tide and spread out over its mud flats when the tide came in. Cambridge was left as a generally low and marshy place.

There were no rocky hills within what are now the city limits because the soft slate of the subsoil had yielded readily to the immense force of the glaciers. The protuberances that remained had been formed by deposits of glacial drift on low rocky knobs. These hills, which the geologists call "drumlins," had the characteristic rounded profile of most of the islands in Boston Harbor and of Beacon Hill in Boston. Cambridge's drumlins are so modest as to be nearly imperceptible beneath the contemporary crust of buildings and streets. Part of Harvard occupies a low drumlin, and there is a higher one in East Cambridge. That one, though only sixty-five feet above sea level, was observed by Generals George Washington and Israel Putnam to be of strategic value. On it they placed a fort which historians deem significant in forcing the British evacuation of Boston in 1776. The Harvard Observatory rests on a ridge formed by the advance of ice over a sandy plain; and Gallows Hill, nearby, is slightly over ninety-nine feet, the highest point in Cambridge.

Perhaps some day archeologists will decide which men first laid eyes on Cambridge. According to legend, around the year 990 the vessel of the Viking Bjärne, son of Herjulf, fell victim to an adverse wind from Greenland and sought shelter in Boston Harbor. The story says he was followed by Leif, son of Eric the Red; Leif's brother Thorvald; Thorfinn Karlsefne with three ships; and still other adventurers. Some of the Norsemen are reputed to have sailed up the Charles River and built houses in Cambridge. The presumed site of their settlement shifts around in Cambridge lore, for no definite traces have ever been discovered. But the myth seems within possibility and brushes the early history of Cambridge with an aura of fantasy absent from Puritan chronicles.

The voyages of later explorers are better documented. Giovanni da Verrazano piloted a French-sponsored expedition which explored the North American coast from Carolina to Nova Scotia; apparently he was more impressed by the Hudson River than the Charles. Samuel de Champlain arrived in the vicinity in 1605 and found it to his liking. Had not his sponsors overruled him, the French might have colonized the Charles valley before the English. In April 1614, Captain John Smith visited the Maine coast in a whaling ship. His travels took him south to Massachusetts and, since he was looking for gold and copper as well as whales, he spent some time ashore. Two years later Smith published his first account of the Massachusetts coast. He also produced a map of the New England coastline, from Maine to Cape Cod, which he presented to Prince Charles. The Prince was impatient with Smith's snarl of Indian place names. And so a curving river which Smith had called "Massachusets" became the River Charles.

Captain Smith loved what is now Massachusetts and became an ardent advocate of its colonization. "The Paradise of all those parts," he called it. People who accused Smith of exaggerating or lying in order to advance the cause of settlement

CAMBRIDGE RECONSIDERED

John Winthrop (1588-1649), first Governor of the Massachusetts Bay Colony. He and his assistants chose the site of Cambridge. This portrait by an unknown artist hangs in the Massachusetts State House in Boston.

underestimated the fairness of a New England spring and a land little abused by man. Smith reported abundant fresh water streams and

—currants, mulberries, vines, gooseberries, plums, walnuts, chestnuts, pumpkins, strawberries, beans, peas, and maize;

—oaks, firs, pines, and other trees yielding wood for building and fuel;

—eagles, hawks, cranes, geese, ducks, turkeys, dew-doppers (most likely the dufflehead duck), and many other birds "whose names I know not";

—moose, deer, bears, wolves, foxes, and otters;

—seas and rivers teeming with fish.

Such abundance could not fail to arouse the envy of people who had been raised where almost every square foot of soil had submitted to the hand of man, where timber had been in short supply for centuries, and where grazing animals prevented cut forests from replenishing themselves. "Heer," Smith promised, "nature and liberty affords us that freely, which in England we want, or it costeth us dearly."

Smith also wrote encouragingly about the New England Indians, or "savages," as he called them. No doubt his past experiences with Pocahontas sweetened his attitude to the North American inhabitants. He found them a "goodly, strong, and well-proportioned people," who enjoyed excellent health. Passing south along the coast he saw "great troupes" of Indians and large corn fields. His encounters with the Indians were usually satisfactory and caused him to arrive at the opinion that the "savage," if discreetly handled, might render valuable assistance to settlers on these shores—a remark that proved prophetic in the case of the Pilgrims who landed at Plymouth in 1620. Smith, however, during a second voyage to New England in 1616, was disturbed to note that the Indian population had been reduced, apparently by some "plague" (probably measles or smallpox caught from white men).

Lacking specificity, Smith's descriptions did not tell much to Thomas Graves, who built his house in 1629 on the drumlin that is now part of East Cambridge, or to Governor John Winthrop and a delegation in December 1630 when they selected the site for what would become Old Cambridge. The Charles River emptied gracelessly into the Back Bay, the tide-raked body of water which ultimately was filled in to create the Back Bay section of Boston. The Charles and the bay met the Cambridge shore at marshes. Graves' land became an island at high tide. Large areas of what is now Cambridgeport were also subject to tidal and seasonal flooding. At that time the Massachusetts Bay Colony consisted of only four organized settlements—Salem, Boston, Charlestown, and Watertown—all of them tiny and brand-new. Fearing that the settlements in Boston and Charlestown were dangerously exposed to the ocean, Governor Winthrop and his assistants determined to find an inland site which could be fortified against naval raids and there to establish their capital.

They were efficient people who wasted little time in deliberation. According to Winthrop's diary on December 14, 1630, the committee scratched from its list the present site of Roxbury (on the inland side

THE FIRST IMMIGRANTS

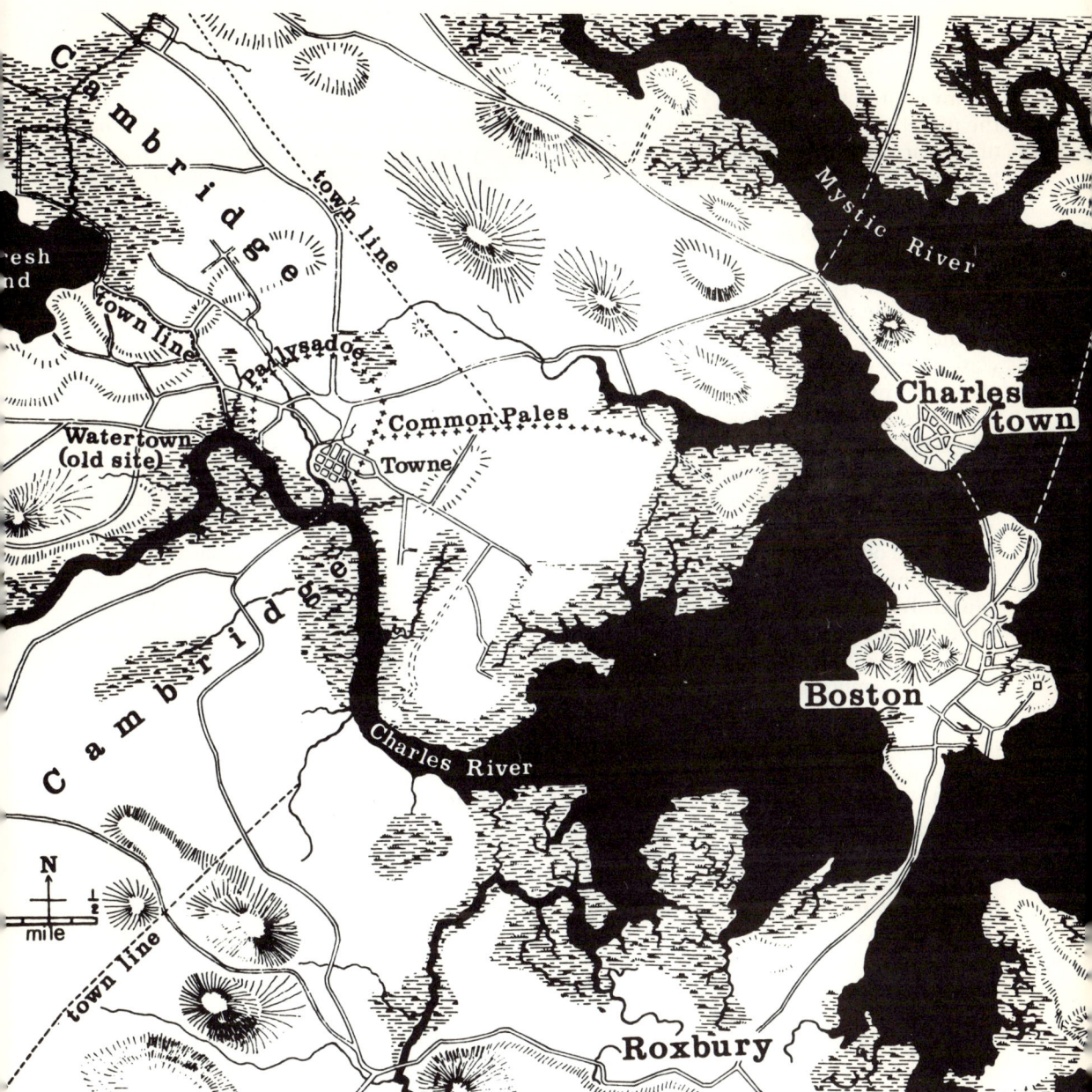

Old Cambridge and environs around 1640. The village itself, protected by its fortification called the "Pallysadoe," is labeled "Towne." But the whole Town of Cambridge then stretched many miles into the wilderness and even included the present-day Brighton and Newton, south of the Charles. Dotted lines in water are ferry routes. Notice that Boston was then almost an island. What now is East Cambridge appears as a hill surrounded by tidal marshes and protruding toward Charlestown.

of Boston's peninsula neck) owing to a shortage of fresh water. Such was the urgency of the matter, however, that they reconvened a week later in Watertown on the upper Charles "and there, upon a view of a place a mile beneath the town, all agreed it a fit place for a fortified town." Just why they objected to Watertown itself is not entirely clear. Presumably they thought it too far from Boston. Instead they had fixed upon a spot five miles upriver from Boston at the entrance of a creek near the northernmost bend of the Charles. There was plenty of fresh water, the river abounded in fish and oysters, and the land was covered with meadows and trees. In this last respect, the site had a distinct edge on Boston, which was unwooded. Though this barrenness had initially been calculated as an advantage because forests harbored wolves and other animal nuisances, the Boston colonists suffered through the first winter for want of fuel. The colony's fathers, having chosen the location of their "new wooded town," named it Newtowne. That was Cambridge's original name.

The decision to erect a fortified town inland suggests that the Puritans feared their king, and possibly the French, more than they did the Indians. The "savages" were scarce in Cambridge in 1630. They may have once lived out at Graves' Neck, but there were no Indian settlements when the colonists arrived. Two perennially feuding tribes lived on the two sides of the Charles. But most of those on the Cambridge side lived farther north, near the Menotomy River and Mystic Pond. Their chieftess, or squaw-sachem, had her wigwam on the west side of that pond. Indians sometimes traversed the new settlement on their way to the river to gather oysters, but there is no record that they bothered the Cambridge colonists or vice versa. The colonists took legal precautions to avoid territorial disputes should the "savages pretend right of inheritance to all or any part of the lands." In 1640, after the village had been occupied for nine years, the squaw-sachem received the sum of ten pounds and the promise of a coat every winter of her life—a slightly better price than the Dutch paid for Manhattan.

Notwithstanding the act of depriving the Indians of their native lands by exploiting their innocence, the Cambridge colonists stayed on good terms with them and treated them much more indulgently than they did non-Calvinist Christians. The Indian heathens, after all, might be candidates for conversion. The first missionary efforts were not encouraging. Winthrop complained that the Indians' usual answer when they were put in mind of God was "Me no know God." Later attempts, notably those of the Reverend John Eliot, were more successful, probably because he dealt respectfully with the Indians and studied their language. (He even translated the Bible into the Massachusetts Indian tongue.) But the Indians contracted European diseases more readily than religious fervor. Epidemics of measles and smallpox reduced their numbers disastrously. In 1646 Eliot wrote of the Indians as "a remnant." He said "there be but few that are left alive from the plague and the pox, which God sent into those parts."

Most Americans have suffered textbook accounts of the New England Puritans. The Indians and the witches of Salem appeal more to the youthful imagination than the prose of Cotton Mather or the dark paintings of Puritans who gave the impression of having been afflicted with permanent indigestion. History handled the Puritans roughly and long ago portrayed them as bigots, uncharitable Christians, and unadmirable representatives of the unique form of government which they initiated in the New England colonies. There is truth in most of the criticisms. But the stereotype of the Puritan—a skinny, prudish, narrow-minded sourpuss—subtracts the part from the whole at the expense of his character.

As religious dissenters, the Puritans were widely regarded as troublemakers in England. Charles I, who took the throne in 1625, loved them not, for he justifiably feared the political implications of religious doctrines which invested the power of decision in the congregation. Even less were the Puritans loved by William Laud, the Bishop of London, who determined to weed out

Calvinist upstarts from the Church of England by persecution. As Laud and his henchmen gained favor with the King, non-conforming Protestants grew insecure. But no matter how bad things were—and for most of the Puritans who joined Winthrop, they were not *that* bad—it required extraordinary courage to exchange the familiarity of home for a remote destination inhabited, John Smith notwithstanding, by savages of questionable intentions. Men usually stay with the devil they know.

The Puritans who bought shares in the Massachusetts Bay Company and followed Winthrop and Deputy-Governor Thomas Dudley to New England were gentry, a literate, often sophisticated people who knew what they were getting into. They had heard about the numerous deaths among the Pilgrims during the first winter at the Plymouth Plantation. They knew, too, that they would find ferocious beasts and a climate far more severe than the one they were leaving. They expected to clear the land, plant crops, build homes, and forage for fuel. They anticipated a future of danger and discomfort. Thus, along with an obstinate desire to practice their religion freely and the commercial inspiration of the Massachusetts Bay Company, the first settlers had a slight touch of recklessness.

A transatlantic sea voyage in 1630 was no vacation cruise. The *Arbella*, which carried Winthrop, Dudley, and the royal charter of the colony, had an uneventful though rough crossing, but another vessel in the Puritan fleet had fourteen deaths, and a third discharged its settlers in a state of near starvation. Then came the confrontation with the wilderness. Some people perished; a few undoubtedly went mad; others gave up and returned to England. But those who were most fit—physically and psychologically—survived and flourished.

The Puritans subscribed to the doctrines of Calvin, and their obsession with original sin and predestination showed up in many a fire-and-brimstone sermon. *The New England Primer* informed small children that "in Adam's fall we sinned all." Yet the private writings of the settlers reveal a richer Puritan character: shrewdness, practicality, devotion to family, and a touching concern for other members of the community. Occasionally there is a hint of humor. They admired intelligence, culture, and wit.

They were, however, deadly serious about religious matters. It is easy enough to blame the notorious witch trials in Salem upon hysteria whipped up by zealots, but Cantabrigians were not fanatics according to the standards of that time and yet they, too, committed atrocities. It has been a matter of some wonder that people who left their homeland for the sake of religious freedom should turn around and deny that freedom to others. History serves up a long and depressing list of the oppressed who eventually became oppressors.

Thomas Graves received one hundred acres of the peninsula which is now East Cambridge in partial payment for his engineering services in laying out the settlement in Charlestown. The Great Marsh overflowed at high tide and cut off his highlands from the mainland. Graves built a house for his wife, five children, and two servants. They resided there in splendid isolation, probably until 1635 when the house became the property of Atherton Haugh. The estate passed from Haughs to Langdons to Phipses to Richard Lechmere (whose name became attached to it, and thus Graves' Neck became Lechmere's Point), and though the holdings increased, decreased, or were divided among different members of different families, there were never more than two working farms out there until Andrew Craigie began wheeling and dealing in the early nineteenth century. The committee which selected the site for the fortified town in 1630 did not even think about Graves, apparently, and it was only in March 1632, when the boundaries of Charlestown and Newtowne were fixed, that Graves discovered himself to be in Newtowne. Well over a century rolled by before this technicality had perceptible impact on the development of Cambridge.

Upriver at the designated site of Newtowne, things got off to a bad start. Since the community was destined to be the provincial capital, the members of the government had agreed to build homes there in the spring of 1631. For those who already had homes elsewhere, this was a colossal nuisance. So when spring came, only Winthrop, Dudley, and Simon Bradstreet among the officials honored the bargain. The Governor built his house of stone laid with clay instead of lime. He had not completed it by October when a violent rainstorm washed down two sides. Unwilling to build yet another house that winter, he removed to his residence in Boston. Meanwhile his strained relations with Dudley discouraged him from building again. Dudley was displeased with Winthrop's conduct on several counts which he enumerated publicly in the summer of 1632. He made his complaint of the Governor's desertion from Cambridge in an address to the General Court—then, as now, the name of the legislative body of Massachusetts. "So the deputy rose up in great fury and passion," Winthrop noted in his journal, "and the governor grew very hot also, so as they both fell into bitterness." Winthrop retaliated by criticizing Dudley's house for excessive wainscotting and ornament. Winthrop remained in Boston, leaving Dudley and Bradstreet to represent the government in Newtowne. Excluding Winthrop's, ten houses were built in 1631. And in 1632 Anne Bradstreet, Simon's wife and Thomas Dudley's daughter, wrote her first poems in a house on the south side of Harvard Square.

Evidence that the Puritans favored forethought over improvisation can be found in the original disposition of streets and regulations for building. The village was laid out in a careful grid pattern. It turned its back upon the marshy, tidal river and faced inland, the present Harvard Square being its approximate northwest corner. After 1633 a rudimentary building code required roofs to be made of slate or shingles rather than the cheaper but flammable thatch. Aesthetic considerations were not ignored; the order further required that "all houses shall range even and stand just six feet from the street." But even in 1633 a visitor from England—the first tourist?—remarked on the neatness and handsomeness of the settlement and also on the prosperity of its residents. A fortification, called the "Pallysadoe," formed an arc enclosing a thousand acres and the village. Intended to contain the cattle and as a defense against Indians, of whom the settlers were still suspicious, the fortification amounted to willows, stakes, and a trench. (For a complete topographical and architectural description of the village see the work of the Cambridge Historical Commission, *Report Four: Old Cambridge,* 1973.)

English Puritans, encouraged by favorable reports and increasingly uneasy at home, arrived in New England in large numbers, swelling the population of Newtowne and other settlements. In the fall of 1633, the dynamic Thomas Hooker arrived in Boston on the same ship with the equally dynamic John Cotton. The Reverend Mr. Cotton stayed in Boston. The Reverend Mr. Hooker crossed over to Newtowne, taking a large congregation with him. By 1635 there were eighty-six tidy houses. Hooker, however, was unhappy. He used the excuse of a shortage of meadowland to cover his more fundamental discomfort at being anywhere near John Cotton. In 1636 he decamped for Connecticut with his entire flock. The Reverend Thomas Shepard and his followers shortly took their place. Shepard, married to Hooker's daughter, was tempted to follow his father-in-law, but decided to stay.

Old Cambridge around 1670. The Common is shown at top. Wood Street (now Boylston) leads to the Great Bridge, completed in 1662.
   1. Market place, 1635.
   2. Site of first meeting house, 1632.
   3. Town wharf and ferry landing, 1635.
   4. Watch House Hill, site of later meeting houses and now the heart of Harvard Square.
   5. Burying ground.
   6. Harvard College.
   7. Site of proposed fort, never built.
   8. Brook from college yard to Creek Lane.
   9. First school house.
10. First jail.
11. Second jail, 1681.
12. Parsonage, 1670.
13. Barrit's Pond, where Harvard's Holyoke Center now stands.
14. Town spring.

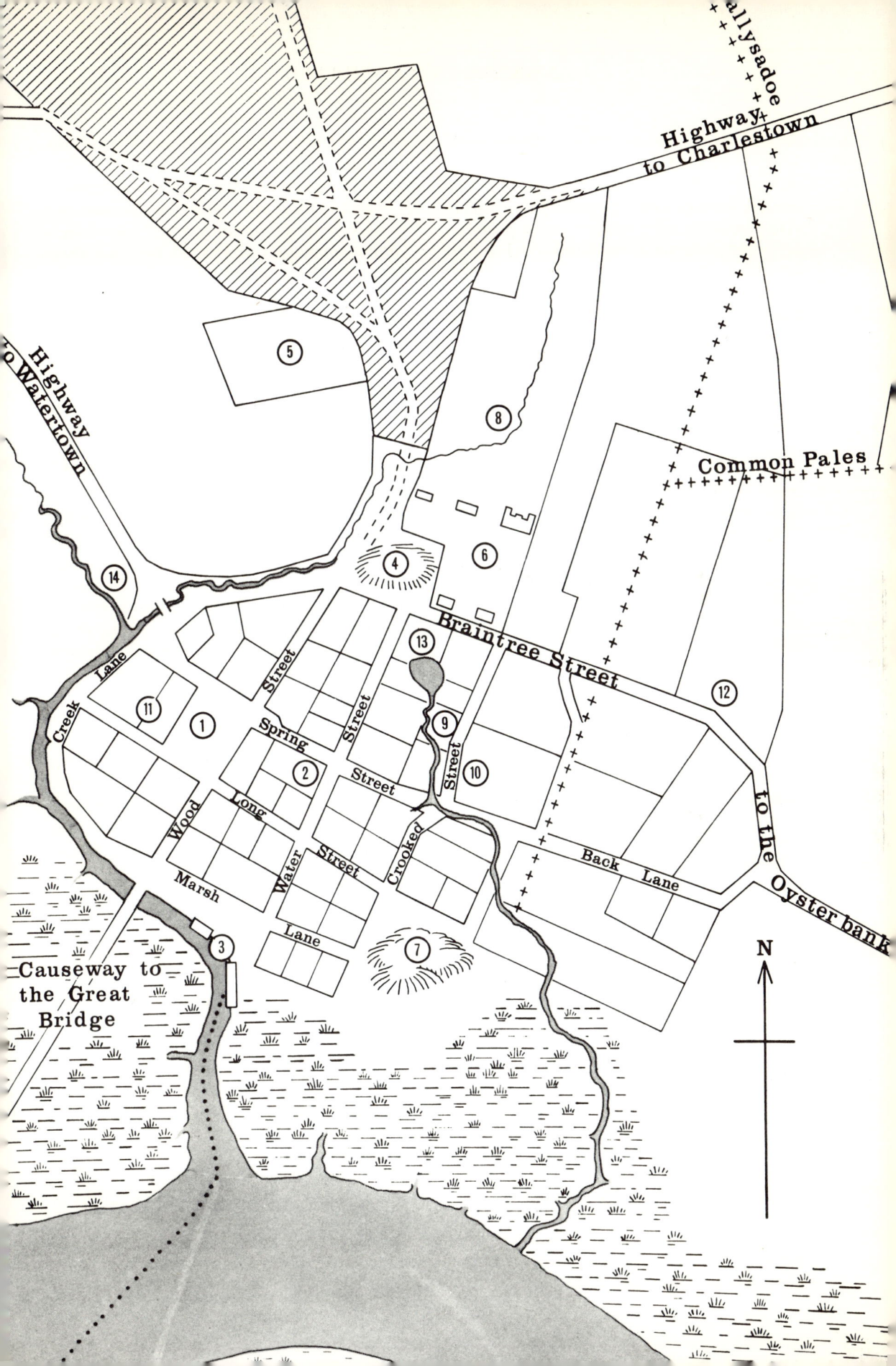

A gentleman of severe views, he became the leading figure in the Newtowne community.

Newtowne never functioned properly as the seat of government it was supposed to be, perhaps because Winthrop declined to live there. The General Court hopped erratically from Boston to Charlestown to Newtowne and back again. Thus Newtowne was just a country village.

In 1636, however, the General Court voted to set aside public funds to support a college, and the following year they determined that the "happy seminary"—in the words of John Cotton—would be established in Newtowne. The village responded in 1638 by granting two and two-thirds acres of land forever for the use of the college. In that same year Newtowne was christened Cambridge in honor of the English university which many of the Puritans, including Shepard, had attended. A building including chambers, studies, a buttery, and a turret on top was erected and pronounced "gorgeous" in disapproving tones by Nathaniel Eaton, the parsimonious individual who was retained as the first instructor, or "Master." A dozen adolescent boys enrolled as the first students. Eaton had a brief, unrewarding career in higher education. In September 1638, one Reverend John Harvard died in Charlestown, leaving half his fortune, his entire library, and ultimately his name to the college. Seldom has so small an endowment (700 pounds and 400 books) brought such fame to its donor. Coincidentally, 1638 was also the year that the General Court came to rest permanently in Boston, ending the suspense over which settlement would be the capital.

In the fall of 1638, at about the time of John Harvard's legacy, the arrival of the first printing press in America north of Mexico reinforced the position of Cambridge as the intellectual center of the colonies. In 1641, Harvard's first president, Henry Dunster, married Elizabeth Glover, widow of the original owner of the press, and because of this the equipment soon found its way into Harvard and eventually became Harvard property. Though presumably Dunster married for love, the press was not the least of the lady's attractions. On her behalf Stephen Daye and his sons had put it into operation in 1638 or 1639. Dunster in 1649 appointed Samuel Green to run it, and Green, who also happened to be commander of Cambridge's militia, managed Harvard's printing shop for forty-three years and raised a whole tribe of illustrious colonial printers. Meanwhile a second press was brought over to Cambridge in 1659 and a third in 1665. Printing did not start in Boston until 1674, and not in any other colony until the 1680s. Thus for about thirty-five years the only printing in the English colonies took place in Cambridge; and every history of printing in the United States must begin with the tiny village on the Charles.

The essential characteristics of pre-revolutionary Cambridge were fixed by 1640. By 1644 the town limits enclosed an area including today's Newton, Brighton, Arlington, Lexington, Bedford, Billerica, and chunks of Belmont and Winchester; this made the town some thirty miles long. As communities developed their own parishes, the boundaries were readjusted, and Cambridge lost territory in accordance with a formula which Charles William Eliot II describes thus: "The optimum area for a town was figured by the time-distance from the meeting house which would permit the farmer to milk his cows, harness old Dobbin, drive his family to the meeting house, endure a two-hour sermon before refreshment at the tavern, and drive home again to milk the cows in the evening." Between 1660 and 1662, the "Great Bridge" was built across the Charles at Old Cambridge, facilitating access to Boston both for the people of Cambridge and for those from the northwest communities. When a high tide washed away part of the bridge in 1685, a ferry substituted until the planks were replaced.

Cambridge residents lived frugally and worked hard. The men were farmers, cattle-raisers, and ministers and teachers in the college. The women wove, sewed, gardened, cooked, and tended to the children. Except for the brief appearance of a surgeon named Abraham Pratt, there was no

THE FIRST IMMIGRANTS

doctor in the town for many years, and the settlers concocted their own remedies for pain and disease, using herbs, wild berries, and roots. Women died in childbirth, and children died in infancy. Contagious disease sometimes wiped out entire families. The children played with dolls, balls, and hoops, but adult games, especially those which either involved or *might* involve gambling, were frowned upon or forbidden. Drunkenness was illegal, but drink was tolerated. An innkeeper named Andrew Belcher received a license to sell bread and beer in 1652. In 1671 he opened the Blue Anchor tavern on the northeast corner of the streets known today as Mount Auburn and Boylston.

The fortifications which had seemed so important in 1630 never amounted to much. The "Pallysadoe" did keep wolves away from the cattle. As for the frightful Indians, those at Mystic Pond to the north voluntarily put themselves under the protection of the English government at Boston in 1644. They never stole from the settlers' homes even when they knew the white men would be at the meeting house. Harvard undertook to educate the "nasty savages," as Charles Chauncy, President Dunster's successor, once called them, and established an Indian College around 1655. Only one Indian, Caleb Cheeshahteaumuck, received a degree; he died of tuberculosis a year later. The experiment failed, perhaps for want of mutual enthusiasm, and in 1665 the Indian College building was turned over to Samuel Green's printing shop.

Mr. Elijah Corlett had apparently run a school for an undetermined number of

The parsonage, built in 1670. For location see No. 12 in map of Old Cambridge, page 15. You are looking approximately east. The first occupant was the Rev. Urian Oakes. He was not only Cambridge's minister but also served as Harvard president from 1675 until his death in 1681. This drawing was made much later (artist unknown). In the background is the house of Francis Dana, built in 1785.

years before 1643 when, in compliance with the General Court's compulsory education act of the previous year, Cambridge opened its first public grammar school, also under the supervision of Mr. Corlett. Though education was not compulsory for girls, they were permitted to attend the school in the summer. Also in 1643, Cambridge became the "shire" town, or county seat, of Middlesex County, by order of the General Court. Legal business was brisk. The court records contain many cases of fornication, adultery, wanton dalliance, unseemly behavior, unchaste words, absence from church, drunkenness, swearing, and breaking the sabbath. Take the case of hapless James Luxford, who committed bigamy in 1639—he had left one wife in England and married a second in Massachusetts. He paid a fine of £100 and spent time in the stocks. Four months later he was convicted of forgery and lying and sentenced to be bound at the whipping post and to have his ears amputated. Apparently Luxford left town soon after receiving his punishment. By 1655 a house of correction—Puritan euphemism for a jail—existed to house criminal offenders. The condemned met their maker on Gallows Hill, north of the present Linnaean Street.

Religious, civic, and college affairs were woven together in one fabric, and it was difficult to determine which thread went where. The meeting house, the "First Church," stood on today's Dunster Street, not far from Dudley's house. A drum was beaten to call the meetings until the village acquired a bell. The whole of Cambridge worshipped there on Sunday. In 1637, the first synod of the churches of the colony gathered there. Anne Hutchinson was tried there for sedition the same year and banished from the colony. And there, in 1642, Harvard held its first commencement exercises. Most important, the town meeting gathered there to decide the affairs of Cambridge. This was a restricted group, comprised of property owners in "good standing" with the church. The town meeting chose "Selectmen" who ran the town. Power was concentrated heavily in the hands of the minister. Furthermore, that the citizens shared the Calvinist assumptions about the close relation between church and state made the business of local government relatively simple. The town meeting may have been democracy by the standards of the Stuart kings, who were nervous over the power of the Puritan congregations, but it was a long way from the practice of democracy in the twentieth century.

The early Cambridge Puritans, like those in many other New England parishes, dreaded the devil and heresy more than Indians or disease. A Cambridge woman named Kendall picked up the child of Goodman Jennison of Watertown and kissed it. The child grew pale and died a few hours later, and the "witch" was hanged on Gallows Hill. In 1654 Henry Dunster was forced from his post as president of Harvard for publicly denouncing the practice of infant baptism. Cambridge ran the Quakers out of town. When Elizabeth Horton cried in the streets that the Lord was coming with fire and sword to judge the citizens of Cambridge, they flogged her and had her dragged out of town at the rear of a cart. Benanuel Bowers, who offered the starving Elizabeth a glass of milk, was fined five pounds for his display of Christian charity.

Benanuel, however, was a fighter and perhaps represented the Cambridge spirit better than his oppressors. Again and again he was hauled into court and fined—for staying away from church, for entertaining Quakers, for refusing to pay fines. He went to jail for over a year. There, to console himself, he wrote defiant verses, for which he was fined again. Released in 1677, he went to church, jumped up on a pew, and complained of the abuses he had suffered. The constables came and dragged him from the church. Like William Lloyd Garrison, the abolitionist of two centuries later, he was *heard*.

3

Inching toward Independence

While Cambridge absorbed itself in the business of settlement and defense against real or imagined enemies, a series of events occurred in England which reverberated in the Massachusetts colony. From 1629 to 1640, Charles I experimented with absolutism and tried to rule without Parliament. Archbishop Laud accumulated power, the breach between Anglicans and Puritans cracked wide open, and religion and politics became curiously embroiled. The people had to choose between Anglican Royalists and Puritan Parliamentarians.

The two factions fought a four-year civil war (1642-1646), a scrambled affair with much aimless marching about, and the Puritans emerged victorious under the leadership of Oliver Cromwell. King Charles was tried and executed in 1649. After Cromwell's demise in 1658, his son failed to fill his boots and, two years later, the English decided to restore the Stuart monarchy in the person of Charles II, who was welcomed home with delirious demonstrations. The new King, supported by a Parliament now more Anglican than Puritan, ruled in the tradition of his father, and Protestant radicals once more came under attack.

Massachusetts followed this saga very closely, though learning of events two or three months after they had taken place. The legal and cultural bonds between the colonists and England were very strong. New Englanders, naturally, sympathized with Cromwell. The Reverend Thomas Shepard's half-brother Samuel was among those who returned to England to serve under Cromwell; so was another Cambridge man, George Cooke. But such sympathies had reasonable limitations. Cromwell's pet project was to people the newly acquired island of Jamaica with New Englanders, and to this end he enlisted Daniel Gookin of Cambridge to entice them to warmer climes. But they were satisfied where they were and respectfully declined. After the coronation of Charles II, two of the judges who had ordered his father's beheading turned up in Cambridge where Gookin gave them shelter and then spirited them away to New Haven only a few days before orders for their arrest arrived from England.

The Restoration brought a number of measures designed to put the American colonies more securely under the royal thumb. The Massachusetts Bay Company, which had governed its own affairs under its charter, most sincerely resented these measures, particularly the Navigation Acts restricting colonial trading practices. The inhabitants of Cambridge, along with those of several other towns, petitioned the King against being "subjected to the arbitrary power of any who are not chosen by this people according to theire patent." The Cambridge document, dated August 17, 1664, predated the American Revolution by more than a century; but now the theme had been sounded.

The petitions achieved nothing except to alert the King to the independent and insolent character of his subjects in Massachusetts and, therefore, to provoke more repressive measures. Meanwhile, the colonial government split into two opinions on how far to press its charter. The Cambridge deputies, led by Gookin and Deputy-Governor Thomas Danforth, took the radical position—as Cambridge people have often done throughout their history—and lost. The English annulled the company charter in 1684 and made Massachusetts a royal colony. Charles II died in 1685 and was succeeded by James II, no improvement. In 1686 Sir Edmund Andros arrived from England to assume the colonial governorship.

Massachusetts despised Andros and the loss of independence which he represented. Cambridge had a special hatred for him because his secretary, Edward Randolph, tried to grab 700 acres of Cambridge land, and Andros would not lift a finger to stop him. On April 18, 1689, prompted by the news that Prince William of Orange had landed in England from Holland and that Stuarts no longer held the throne, Massachusetts citizens rebelled against the Governor. Andros had insufficient forces to resist. In Boston he fled into the fort on Fort Hill (south of Beacon Hill) but had to surrender. The rebels locked him in jail, and soon he retreated from the colonies in disgrace. The charter was revived, though never did the colonists regain all the liberties they had enjoyed in the early years. Danforth was reinstated as Deputy-Governor, Simon Bradstreet as Governor—he lived to a colossal age—and Cambridge was ecstatic. The villagers pledged their persons and estates in case the English sent a punitive expedition. The pledge would be honored by their descendants in 1775.

During the eighteenth century, the colonists became progressively more attentive to worldly affairs. The selection of John Leverett as Harvard president in 1707 was symptomatic of a change of intellectual standards. Leverett, a former tutor at the college and a layman known to have kind feelings toward the Church of England, had once been accused of subversion by those pillars of puritanism, Cotton and Increase Mather. Though the Mathers campaigned actively against him, the Fellows of Harvard College elected Leverett by a comfortable margin.

Cambridge matured in the eighteenth century. The boundaries shrank. Having lost Shawshin (Billerica) and Cambridge Village (Newton) in the seventeenth century, Cambridge lost Cambridge Farms (Lexington) in 1713—a matter of small consequence to the village clustered around Harvard. In Old Cambridge proper, the streets bore the quaint names of the original settlement—names like Creek Lane, Long, Crooked, Wood, and Spring, which suggest that the inhabitants were not disposed to undue haste in honoring their dead leaders. Cambridge's population did not increase dramatically. Nevertheless, by mid-century the sleepy little farming village with a college had developed into an elegant, sophisticated village—with a college.

Money came to Cambridge and with money came luxury. Some of the money belonged to local families, such as Brattle and Foxcroft, who had made good and grown weary of Puritanism. Most of it was new. Vassalls, Inmans, Phipses, and Lechmeres were at first not Cambridge people. Their wealth came from service to the King, the Boston shipping houses, West Indies plantations, and the slave trade—in those days entirely respectable. They conducted their affairs in Boston and discovered Cambridge conveniently nearby. They were attracted by the "country"— large tracts of land on which they could create graceful lawns and gardens in the style of the English landed gentry whom they emulated. Inmans bought property north of the present Massachusetts Avenue, behind the spot where City Hall stands now. Francis Foxcroft came into possession of the Danforth estate by marriage to Thomas Danforth's daughter, Elizabeth. Spencer Phips purchased the old Graves-Haugh place out in East Cambridge, but evidently its remoteness did not suit him. When a large estate between the present Arrow Street and the river came on the market, Phips bought it, moved into the house, and converted it into the social center of Cambridge. But the most famous estates were those on the road to Watertown, west of the Cambridge Common. This is today's Brattle Street, still one of the most handsome streets in the United States.

The new residents delighted in a display of wealth. They built mansions and created manicured landscapes, planted with exotic trees and shrubs imported from England and France. Not all of their embellishments were tasteful. The Phips estate, for example, guarded its entrances with life-like wooden Indians decorated with feathers and bows and arrows. The wealthy women wore finery from London and affected courtly manners. The "aristocrats" had liveried servants, rode in gorgeous carriages, and attended balls with much gaiety and drinking. Their ranks were closed, and

INCHING TOWARD INDEPENDENCE

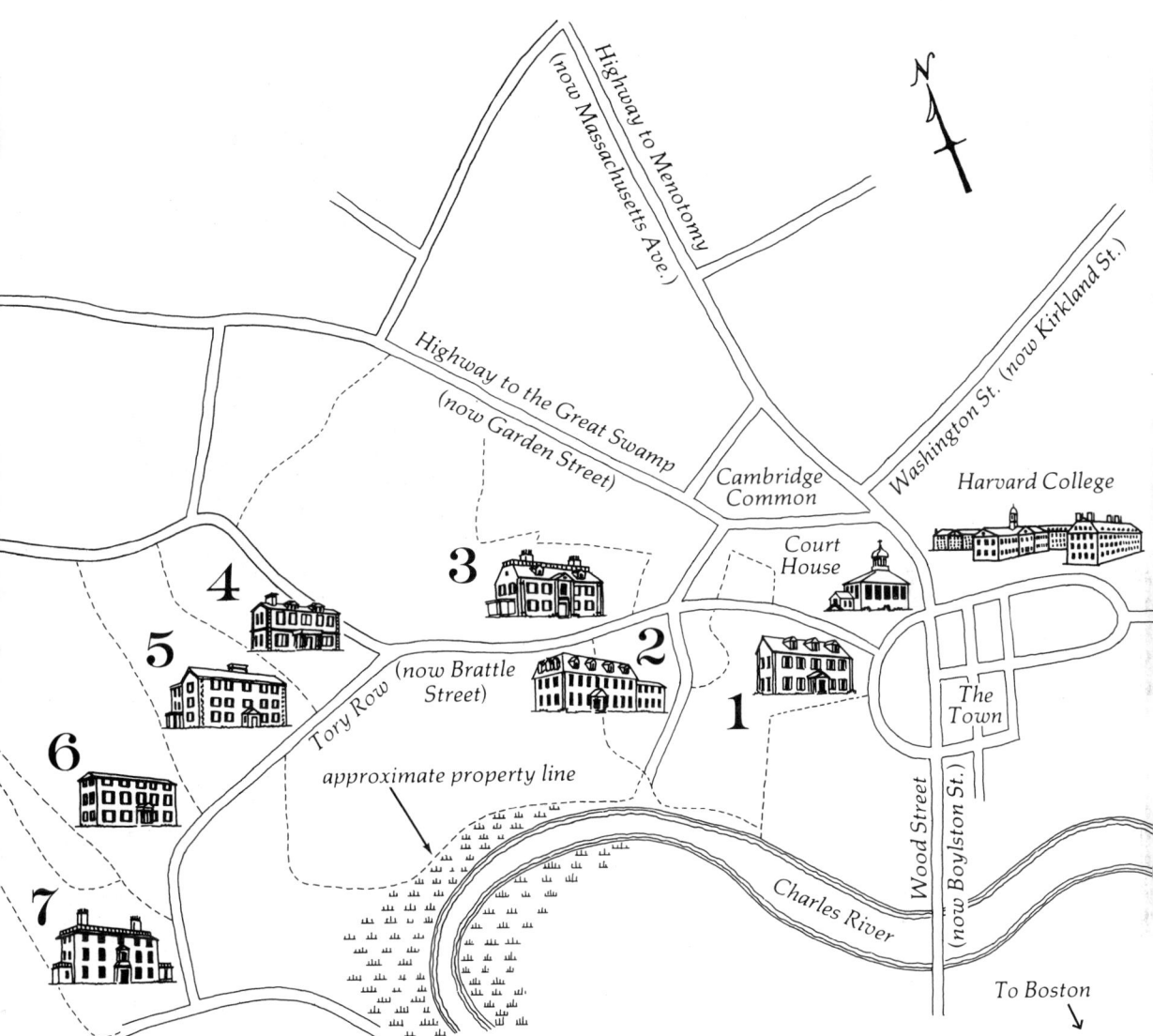

Tory Row estates, 1774. "Menotomy," mentioned at top, is the old name for Arlington. The numbered estates are as follows:
1. General William Brattle's home. A portrait of him appears later in this chapter. The house now is occupied by the Cambridge Center for Adult Education.
2. Mrs. Henry Vassall's home, later used as medical headquarters for Washington's army.
3. Home of John Vassall, Jr., later General Washington's headquarters. A picture of it appears in Chapter 4.
4. Judge Jonathan Sewall's home.
5. Judge Joseph Lee's home, now the home of the Cambridge Historical Society.
6. Colonel George Ruggles's home.
7. Lieutenant-Governor Thomas Oliver's home, "Elmwood," pictured later in this chapter.

The Rev. East Apthorp, first rector of Christ Church.

Modern picture of Christ Church on Garden Street, built in 1760. In foreground is the Old Burying Ground, more than a century older than the church. At upper left is a corner of Harvard's Larsen Hall, built more than two centuries after the church.

the genealogies of these dozen or so Cambridge families are intermingled.

Seventeenth-century Cambridge would have kicked people out for lesser extravagances. Eighteenth-century Cambridge endured the excesses of the affluent. The descendants of the Puritans, however, did not approve of what they judged as loose moral behavior and wanton display of wealth. They were also uneasy with the Royalist political sympathies and the Anglican religious doctrines to which the rich subscribed. Thus the Road to Watertown earned the name of "Tory Row." And when East Apthorp, the first rector of the new Episcopal church (Christ Church, built in 1760), moved into his stately new residence between the present Plympton and Linden Streets, the villagers dubbed it "The Bishop's Palace." After Apthorp returned to England in 1764, Boston merchant John Borland bought the house and kept the Tory tradition.

Though the Tories were only about 10 percent of the Cambridge populace, their influence in the village outweighed their numbers. On the whole, it was a good influence. The Tories brought variety, vitality, and worldliness into a society which had been monotonous, uniform, and stodgy. Cambridge slowly relaxed, like a woman loosening her corset. That does not mean that moral or intellectual standards deteriorated. As Samuel Sewall had observed in 1726, *"Venimus ipsam, Cantabrigiam ad stabiliendos, et corrigendos mores"*— "Cambridge, of course, is still the place to come to establish correct behavior and usage." Still, the mood was definitely more expansive. From the *Boston Gazette*, April 26, 1725, came the notice "to all Gentlemen and others, that there is to be Thirty Pounds in money run for on Thursday, the 13th of May next at 9 o'clock, by Six Horses, Mares, or Geldings. Two miles between Menotomy & Cambridge...." A horse race in Cambridge? The founding fathers would have fainted.

In general the Tories were not civic-minded people, except for their service to Harvard College. They kept their tight circle and were devoted to finance, foppishness, and fashion. One exception was John Vassall, Sr. He was a Selectman in 1739 and 1740, but Samuel Whittemore—currier, deacon, and dealer in real estate—pronounced publicly that Vassall was no more fit to discharge said trust than the horse that he rode. Vassall sued for defamation of character and lost both the suit and the next election. His son, John Vassall, Jr., sat for a while on the eighteenth-century version of the School Committee, and he also paid for the land upon which Christ Church was built.

The 90 percent of the Cambridge inhabitants who were not Tories scarcely lived in luxury, but their life was more comfortable than that of the early settlers. Experience had taught New Englanders to construct weatherproof, snug homes, with clapboard or shingle walls, leaded casement windows, and steep roofs which shed the winter snows. Natural hazards had diminished. Wolves still prowled the forests and upset livestock, but bears were on the decline, and in 1754 the pursuit of a 196-pound bear at Lechmere's Point was a matter of some excitement. There had been no panic about Indians since 1676; the scariest Indians in Cambridge stood in Spencer Phips's front yard.

Contagious disease was scary enough, though. Several smallpox epidemics alarmed Cambridge. The first outbreak, in 1721, caused so many deaths in Boston that the General Court retreated to Cambridge and, even there, convened three miles from the center of town. Harvard dismissed its students briefly in 1730 because of smallpox. A few progressive doctors in Boston and Cambridge experimented with inoculations, but the process was dangerous and many people feared it. (Actual smallpox, not cowpox, was then used as the vaccine.) In June 1740 an epidemic of "throat distemper"—apparently influenza—caused at least half a dozen deaths in as many days. Edward Holyoke, Harvard's president, for whom Holyoke Center in Harvard Square is named, lost his wife and youngest son. Harvard shut down, and commencement was postponed until after the summer recess. A smallpox scare wiped out the commencement of 1752.

Modern picture of Massachusetts Hall, built in 1720, Harvard's oldest surviving structure. A sketch of it, from the other end, appears at the extreme right of the map of Tory Row, page 21.

Many houses were built, rebuilt, or improved between 1700 and the Revolution. In addition, a number of public buildings appeared: Christ Church, the second courthouse and then the third, the third meeting house and then the fourth, and five Harvard buildings. By 1750 Harvard Square was nearly surrounded by buildings. The greatest property disaster occurred on the night of January 24, 1764, when a fire erupted in Harvard Hall. The building was being used during the winter vacation for sessions of the General Court owing to a smallpox scare in Boston. Aroused by the meeting-house bell, Cambridge inhabitants rushed from their homes into a snowstorm and lined up in bucket brigades. They saved Massachusetts and Hollis halls, but Harvard Hall was lost. The fire destroyed the college library of 5,000 volumes, including John Harvard's literary legacy, along with precious portraits and science exhibits.

Commercial and professional activities prospered. A list of tradesmen from the 1750s shows a barber, brickmaker, cooper, currier, distiller, glazier, hatter, saddler, two blacksmiths, five carpenters, three tailors, and three tanners—also three lawyers. The Blue Anchor Tavern, having passed from the Belcher family and then through many hands, came to rest in 1749 with Ebenezer Bradish, who transferred the sign to a new location on Wood Street (now Boylston) and had a flourishing trade. But he had competition from numerous innkeepers and licensed retailers who satisfied the communal thirst of a town that was much less temperate than in Puritan days.

Occasional commotions ruffled the serene surface of Cambridge. There was a minor scandal in 1721 when two men were accused of double-voting during the election of a representative. Both denied their guilt under oath and the matter appears to have been dropped. Professor John Winthrop, who was a descendant of the first Governor and was Hollis Professor of Mathematics and Natural History, more distinguished than any Harvard faculty member before him, kept a diary in which he recorded the last public execution in Cambridge on September 18, 1755: "Two negroes belonging to Capt. Codman executed for petit treason, for murdering their said master by poison. They were drawn upon a sled to the place of execution; and Mark, a fellow about 30, was hanged; and Phillis, an old creature, was *burnt to death*."

Winthrop also noted an earthquake on June 3, 1744: "½ after 10 A.M. a earthquake which shook the houses and much surprised the people in the meetinghouse occasioned a great number of them to get out in speed. The night following there were 3 or 4 rumbles of earthquakes."

The earthquake only rattled the inhabitants of Cambridge. The Stamp Act of 1765 shook them to the bone. This act of Parliament required the purchase of tax stamps for pamphlets, licenses, ship's papers, newspapers, insurance policies, and other printed matter, and thus imposed the first direct taxation upon the American colonies. Down in Virginia, Patrick Henry made an inflammatory speech, and not long afterward, back in Boston, a mob destroyed the home of Lieutenant-Governor Thomas Hutchinson, Harvard 1727, who had demonstrated his willingness to enforce the Stamp Act. Cambridge, not yet to the point of violence, refused to contribute a share of the compensation for Hutchinson's losses. In October 1765 the town meeting ordered its representatives "by no means whatsoever to do any one thing" that might aid the act in its operation.

So resolute was American resistance to the act that within less than a year British merchants were losing money and moved for its repeal, which took place in 1766. But George III and Parliament proceeded with their efforts to squeeze and subdue the colonies. One repressive measure followed another. The crown had badly misjudged the temper of the colonies. Each new offensive law unified them and made them more stubborn. The Americans had become a self-assured people, accustomed to managing their own affairs. They resented being treated like naughty school children. Violence increased. In Boston on March 5, 1770, a boisterous crowd gathered around a British sentry; he called for help; a musket volley killed five citizens; and the incident entered history as the Boston Massacre. Cambridge and other communities immediately signaled their sympathies. A serious uprising was prevented when Hutchinson, by this time Acting Governor (he would take the oath of office as Governor in March 1771), removed the British troops to islands in Boston harbor.

Yet most Americans were reluctant revolutionaries. They asked only for a redress of grievances and persisted in their loyalty to King George. The Cambridge town meeting patiently stated its woes in petition after petition. In 1772 the Cantabrigians complained, "We have been sighing and groaning under oppression for a number of years; our natural and charter rights are violated in too many instances here to enumerate; our money extorted from us, and appropriated to augment our burdens."

The colonists' sense of dissatisfaction gradually evolved into a rebellious attitude. In November 1772, Samuel Adams, Harvard 1740, organized the Committee of Correspondence in Boston. Cambridge promptly responded with a local Committee of Correspondence of its own. The town meeting instructed the committee to advise the Bostonians that, if the grievances continued to be ignored, the colonists "must overthrow, the happy civil constitution of this Province. It is with the greatest pleasure we now inform you that we think the meeting was as full as it has been ... for a number of years, if not fuller; and that the people discovered a glorious spirit, like men determined to be free."

The British blundered ahead. The Tea Act came next. Though the tax was small, the violation of colonial rights which it represented was large. Cambridge disclosed its readiness to resist the new outrage and announced that "this town can no longer stand idle spectators." Cambridge men helped plot the Boston Tea Party of 1773. The British punished Boston with the Port Bill, which forbade the loading or unloading of ships until the East India Company had been paid for the tea which the patriots had dumped overboard. Cambridge, lacking a port of its own, was equally affected, and pledged to aid the beleaguered Bostonians.

In May 1774 Parliament effectively annulled the Massachusetts charter by replacing officials elected by the colonists with a crown-appointed body called the Mandamus Council. Among the thirty-six members were three Cambridge men: Thomas Oliver, Samuel Danforth, and Joseph Lee. Governor Hutchinson dissolved the General Court on June 17, leaving the Mandamus Council in control of the government. On August 8 in Salem, the council met for the first time. At this point, the struggle between arbitrary power and the colonists' desire for liberty became intense.

At 4:30 a.m. on September 1, 1774, British soldiers under orders from General Thomas Gage, the military governor in Boston, raided the powderhouse in a part of Charlestown that is now in Somerville and seized the entire store of gunpowder. Another detachment entered nearby Cambridge and removed two field pieces. Within hours the entire Boston area had heard of the incident and believed that a British military attack was imminent. Citizens hastily gathered arms, ammunition,

William Brattle (1706-1776), as painted by John Singleton Copley in 1756. A general in the militia, sometimes called "Brigadier Paunch," Brattle switched to the Loyalist side and in 1776 left Boston with the British troops. He died in Halifax.

and provisions. William Brattle, prominent Cambridge citizen and militia officer, known for wavering political affections, was widely suspected of precipitating the raids by informing the British of the contents of the powderhouse; and the Mandamus Council was thought to have conspired in the plans.

That night, Cambridge citizens were at last in a belligerent mood. A volatile crowd, which a Boston newspaper described as "boys and negroes," surrounded the Tory Row house of Jonathan Sewall, the Massachusetts Attorney-General. A gun was said to have been fired from one of the windows and the demonstrators shattered some glass. The assemblage dispersed before further damage occurred. But the following morning, September 2, several thousand indignant people from Cambridge and neighboring places converged in front of the courthouse on the west side of Harvard Square. Mandamus Councilmen Danforth and Lee emerged and stood on the steps to address the crowd. Poor

Danforth, one of a long line of prominent Cambridge Danforths, a 78-year-old judge with decades of creditable service behind him, no doubt spoke truthfully when he claimed he had accepted the crown's appointment solely to serve the people; the crowd's hostility bewildered him. Both he and Lee resigned from the Council. David Phips, the county sheriff, vowed not to enforce the new acts of Parliament. But Phips, Royalist to the marrow, soon chose to leave the colonies.

The remaining Cambridge member of the Mandamus Council, Thomas Oliver, was Lieutenant-Governor of Massachusetts. He had hastened to Boston to inform General Gage of the crowd on Cambridge Common and to implore him not to send out any troops. Oliver then returned to Cambridge and, though declining to resign from the Council, promised not to act against the colonists' interests. Meanwhile, however, suspicious activities were observed in the British camp, and rumors flew back to Cambridge that soldiers were preparing to move in on the crowd. In view of this, the Massachusetts men did not believe Oliver's assurances that the British were not coming, and they followed him westward along Tory Row to his mansion "Elmwood," confronted him, and intimidated him into resigning from the council. Ten days later he moved his family and furnishings out of town, and eventually he went to Bristol, England.

As for William Brattle, few believed his denial of his role in the powderhouse affair. He, too, found it expedient to leave Cambridge and retreat behind the British lines in Boston. The political climate in Cambridge became such that a number of other Royalists did the same. Harvard boys, who should have been memorizing Vergil, were distracted by current events. After March 1, 1775, when patriot students nearly lynched half a dozen Tories who brought tea into Harvard Hall (long since rebuilt after the fire), the faculty had to ban the drinking of tea in order to preserve a semblance of scholarly order.

Not one drop of blood was shed on September 2, 1774, but, had the British troops appeared in Cambridge, the Revolu-

Modern picture of "Elmwood," the estate of Lieutenant-Governor Thomas Oliver, scene of revolutionary excitement in September 1774 and two hundred years later the official residence of Harvard President Derek Bok. It is on Elmwood Avenue just off Brattle Street.

tionary War probably would have started then and there. Indeed, the importance of the happenings that day has led Charles William Eliot II, presiding over the Cambridge Historical Society, to maintain that "the Revolution started in Cambridge in 1774." In any case, the redcoats stayed in Boston and the patriots gained time to prepare themselves for the conflict that now was inevitable.

In 1774, with General Gage and his troops in possession of Boston, Cambridge finally fulfilled the expectations of the Puritan founders by becoming the seat of the Massachusetts government, albeit temporary and provisional. During October the Massachusetts Assembly met at the Cambridge meeting house to appoint committees of safety and supplies, and then again to appoint a committee to watch British troop movements.

On April 18, 1775—the eighty-sixth anniversary of the rebellion against Governor Edmund Andros—colonial spies discovered that General Gage planned to assault the patriots' military stores in Concord. That night Paul Revere and William Dawes galloped off to warn the countryside. While Revere traveled through Charlestown, Dawes took the route along the neck of the Boston peninsula, across the Great Bridge, and through the Cambridge Common before dawn on the 19th. Hearing his call, six Harvard youths slammed their books shut and raced off to join the Minutemen. Meanwhile the first British troops slogged ashore on Lechmere's Point. A second detachment, led by Lord Percy, went the route of Dawes. Cambridge men removed the planks from the Great Bridge, stalling Percy's progress until his soldiers could replace them, and Harvard students misdirected the redcoats.

Bronze horseshoes imbedded in a sidewalk next to the Cambridge Common mark the path which William Dawes took to Lexington in April 1775, arousing the countryside. The Dawes family donated this William Dawes Memorial to the city in 1975 as part of the Bicentennial celebration.

Three black men—Cato Boardman, Cato Stedman, and Cuff Whittemore—marched with the Cambridge militiamen to protect the Concord arsenal. When the British arrived at Lexington at dawn, seventy-seven armed Minutemen greeted them. The British killed eight and wounded ten, and proceeded to Concord. There, they managed to get their hands on some of the munitions they had come for, but they were met by a large body of patriots at North Bridge and suffered casualties in the clash. The redcoats also were under continual fire on their weary return to Boston. Half a dozen Cambridge men died in skirmishes during the British retreat. Their names: Jason Russell, Jason Winship, Jabez Wyman, John Hicks, Moses Richardson, and William Marcy.

Messengers rode furiously through the countryside, spreading news of the latest events. Volunteers streamed into Cambridge, and within a week the soldiers outnumbered its 1,600 or so residents. The patriots were commanded by General Artemas Ward, a righteous individual who suffered from gallstones and who tried desperately to establish order in the chaotic makeshift camp. Harvard buildings became barracks, and the college moved out to Concord for about a year. Christ Church, symbol of Anglican and Tory arrogance, housed troops from Connecticut. Abandoned Tory mansions served as barracks and hospitals. By May, 16,000 undisciplined soldiers milled around Cambridge, bathing on warm days in the Charles River—often with disregard for modesty—and waiting impatiently for the British to try to break out of Boston. General Israel Putnam, an old Indian fighter with a taste for battle, made camp for 3,000 troops near the site of the present Central Square so as to be close to the action. On June 17, redcoats advanced upon Charlestown where 1,200 patriot troops had occupied and fortified Breed's Hill, and they clashed there in what history calls the Battle of Bunker Hill. Among the patriots was a young apothecary named Andrew Craigie of whom more will be heard later. In the battle, General Gage's soldiers carried the day but suffered tremendous losses.

CAMBRIDGE RECONSIDERED

In 1875 a forlorn Washington Elm stands in Garden Street in front of the First Church, Congregational, which faces the Common. When this legendary tree was finally removed in 1923, cuttings were taken, and a scion was planted in the Common in 1946.

Wadsworth House, built in 1726 and occupied by many Harvard presidents, is the wooden structure with the flag. It stands on Massachusetts Avenue at Harvard Square. It is where George Washington *really* took command of the army in 1775. This 1975 photograph shows a re-enactment of his arrival — a part of Cambridge's Fourth of July parade of that year. Wadsworth House now contains the Harvard alumni offices and *Harvard Magazine*.

INCHING TOWARD INDEPENDENCE

Among the rebels who died was the second in command, Thomas Gardner of Cambridge, a respected citizen and ardent patriot.

George Washington arrived on July 2 as the new Commander-in-Chief of the Continental Army, and now Cambridge was suddenly far more than the military center of New England—it was the headquarters of the whole American war effort. According to legend, Washington assumed his command on July 3 when he inspected the ragged troops beneath an elm tree on the Common. Many people believe by now that the "ceremony" really took place in Wadsworth House, which was then occupied by Harvard's President Samuel Langdon, but the "Washington Elm," which stood in the middle of the intersection of Garden and Mason Streets until it perished in 1923, retained enough sentimental value to be adopted as the city's bicentennial symbol in the 1970s.

Washington was appalled by the dirt and disorder among the troops. General Ward could not tell him how many men were in the camp—18 or 20 thousand, he guessed; eight weeks later Washington knew that he had a force of 13,743 able-bodied men. The plantation owner from Virginia, a man of fastidious habits, remarked in a letter to his cousin that the New Englanders were "an exceedingly dirty and nasty people."

Washington commandeered the mansion of John Vassall, Jr., on Tory Row for his headquarters and got down to the business at hand. His objective was to contain the British in Boston and give them no option but to retreat to England. For the siege of Boston he set his men to erecting a line of fortifications. Those in Cambridge included No. 1 on the river where the Riverside Press later stood; No. 2 on the easterly side of the present Putnam Avenue; a line of several detached forts and redoubts along the summit of Butler's Hill, now called Dana Hill; Fort Putnam, out at Lechmere's Point; and Fort Washington, a three-gun battery at what is now the foot of Albany Street. Fort Washington commanded the Charles River all the way down to Lechmere's Point.

These fortifications were useless without fire power, however, and Washington's most pressing problem was a shortage of weapons and ammunition which put his army in greater peril than either they (or the British) knew. Furthermore his funds had run out, and he feared for his men during the winter. On September 21, he informed the Continental Congress of his grim situation: "The paymaster has not a single dollar in hand; the commissary assures me he has strained his credit, for the subsistence of the army, to the utmost. The Quartermaster General is precisely in the same situation; and the greater parts of the troops are in a state not far from mutiny, upon the deduction from their stated allowance." Washington concluded that if the evils were not remedied, "the army must absolutely break up." The Congress in Philadelphia was alarmed and dispatched Benjamin Franklin and two other delegates to Cambridge to see what could be done. Franklin's committee spent nine days in October conferring with Washington and

Cannon at Fort Washington guards a truck terminal. During the Revolution, however, before the marshes along the Charles were filled, the big guns guarded the river against a British naval raid.

his generals and touring the camp. They concluded by pledging further assistance on behalf of the Continental Congress and accepting Washington's view that the army was in no condition to launch an attack on the British in Boston.

Gunpowder was slowly smuggled into camp during the fall. Then, in January 1776, a 24-year-old colonel named Henry Knox arrived from Fort Ticonderoga, New York, with more than forty cannon which, incredibly, had been drawn over the snow on ox-sleds. The presence of these long-range guns, placed on Dorchester Heights south of Boston, forced the British to evacuate Boston. On March 17, 1776, more than 10,000 redcoats and royalists jammed the decks of British ships bound for Halifax and England. Among them were Lechmeres, Sewalls, and Vassalls. The siege of Boston had ended.

The army and General Washington departed for New York, leaving behind the ravages of eleven months of occupation. Many houses, farms, and roads had been destroyed; the woods had been devastated during the winter; even fenceposts had been torn up for firewood. Cambridge felt relieved to watch the army pull out. The population shrank overnight, Harvard returned from Concord, farmers planted new crops, and people started to clean up the mess while anxiously awaiting the news that the British were defeated and America had won its freedom.

Thus, by the time of the Declaration of Independence, when the Americans made their commitment to an all-or-nothing war, Cambridge had lost its position as military headquarters of the new nation. But nearly all able-bodied men in the village served in the army at one time or another. Their absences caused much heavy work to fall upon Cambridge women and children. Children matured early in those days, without the luxury of prolonged adolescence.

In October 1777 an event on a distant battlefront had a heavy effect on Cambridge. The British general John Burgoyne surrendered his army of 5,700 men at Saratoga, New York. The Americans decided to ship their prisoners back to England on the pledge that they would never again serve against the patriots. Cambridge achieved the dubious honor of being selected as the detention camp—a sort of half-way house. General William Heath, district commander, hastily arranged for the ordinary soldiers to stay in some existing barracks at Prospect and Winter hills (now in Somerville) and for the officers to lodge with civilians—many of whom were less than delighted with the idea.

Burgoyne's exhausted, muddy army limped into town in November, straggling past the deserted Tory houses. Burgoyne was assigned to the "Bishop's Palace," that is, the Apthorp house. The Hessian General, Baron von Riedesel, commander of Britain's German allies, and his family were directed to Jonathan Sewall's vacant mansion on Tory Row following a short, disagreeable term in a barracks. Cambridge crawled with redcoats for a year. Though the enemy was more orderly than the patriot army had been, their good manners were not appreciated. There were several heated exchanges between high-strung citizens and loosely confined prisoners, and one incident resulted in the death of a British officer. A funeral was held in Christ Church, attended by all the British and German officers, and the body of the lieutenant was placed in the Vassall tomb. The ceremony upset Cantabrigians and some of them vandalized the church. A British eyewitness recorded that "the Americans seized the opportunity of the Church being open . . . to plunder, ransack and deface every thing they could lay their hands on, destroying the pulpit, reading-desk and communion-table, and ascending the organ loft, destroyed the bellows and broke all the pipes of a very handsome instrument."

The Baroness von Riedesel, however, had the gift of making the best of a bad situation. She found the accommodations to her liking, in fact downright "agreeable." She amused herself with puttering in the neglected Sewall gardens and listening to gossip about Cambridge's social glories before the Tory luminaries had taken flight. On King George's birthday, this plucky

INCHING TOWARD INDEPENDENCE

Inside Christ Church in 1975, about two centuries after the building's important role during the Revolution.

woman gave a dinner party in his honor. Insulted Cambridge citizens surrounded the house in non-violent protest. On another day, perhaps in a fit of boredom, she engraved her name with a diamond on a windowpane.

In April 1778 Burgoyne left Cambridge under escort with part of his army and went to Rhode Island. The rest of the soldiers were moved south the following November owing to a shortage of provisions in the Boston region. Elsewhere in the colonies, the fighting dragged on for three more years, but Massachusetts remained outside the perimeter of battle. Cambridge prepared for peace and independence—a little overconfidently, perhaps, since military victory was not assured. From September 1779 to May 1780, the Cambridge meeting house in Harvard Square was the site of the convention to frame a constitution for Massachusetts. The constitution was drafted by John Adams and contained several important provisions. For example, it abolished property qualifications for voting and it asserted the right of the people to alter the government. Cambridge ratified the document at a town meeting on May 23, and it has served the Commonwealth ever since. The Massachusetts constitution prepared the way for the United States constitution of 1787.

4

Enter the Speculators

When President Washington visited Harvard in 1789 he found a peaceful, attractive Cambridge whose citizens welcomed him enthusiastically—a scene he probably had trouble reconciling with his memories of disorder and truculence. The Cambridge of 1789 looked pretty much like the pre-war Cambridge of 1775. The old Harvard building called "Stoughton College," whose condition had been worsened by its wartime inhabitants (Washington's troops), had been torn down. No public buildings had been put up because of the financial hard times created by the Revolution and its aftermath. Cosmetically, Cambridge seemed to have returned to its past.

But there was one big difference: the Tories were gone. During the Revolution, their estates had been confiscated by the Commonwealth. In 1783 there had been some discussion about reclamation, but Cambridge was not in a charitable mood, and the town meeting voted unanimously against this proposal. A few Tories contrived to keep land in their families—among them the Brattles. Joseph Lee, who had resigned from the Mandamus Council during the disturbances of September 2, 1774, was considered a harmless gentleman, and his lands had escaped confiscation. He lived quietly in his old house and enjoyed pleasant relations with his neighbors. But the Commonwealth sold the Oliver, Lechmere, Sewall, Phips, and Vassall estates in the village to patriots.

Elmwood, Thomas Oliver's residence, went to Andrew Cabot of Salem in 1779 for £47,000 "lawful money," the inflated paper currency ("Continentals") of the time. Cabot, a real estate speculator, also purchased extensive land on Lechmere's Point with hope of building a bridge from there to Boston. Cabot was not interested in living in Cambridge, only in making money from Cambridge properties. Therefore, in 1787, he sold Elmwood to Elbridge Gerry, originally from Marblehead, Massachusetts.

Elbridge Gerry was one of those persons who had little impact on Cambridge but who was an important national figure. Such individuals turn up frequently in the town's history. Gerry, a gifted man and signer of the Declaration of Independence, was a member of the constitutional convention of 1787 in Philadelphia where he had earned the nickname of "the old Grumbletonian" for challenging the constitution because he feared the concentration of power in federal hands. Said his old friend, John Adams, "he opposed everything he did not propose." Gerry had unorthodox political opinions. He was a Jeffersonian Republican who nevertheless favored Hamilton's fiscal policies. In the presidential election of 1796 he cast his electoral vote for the Federalist John Adams. Adams

Elbridge Gerry: Harvard graduate, signer of the Declaration of Independence, resident of the Cambridge mansion "Elmwood," Massachusetts Governor, and fifth Vice-President of the United States.

sent him to France to negotiate disputes with that country. When Gerry and his fellow commissioners arrived in Paris, three agents (identified in subsequent reports mysteriously as X, Y, and Z) showed up and demanded a loan from the United States and a bribe for Foreign Minister Talleyrand as the price for treaties of commerce and amity. The other two Americans went home in disgust, but Gerry lingered in the hope that he could come to terms with the French. Meanwhile, the "XYZ Affair" created a scandal in the United States. Cambridge, a Federalist stronghold partial to England rather than France, resented the apparent preference that Elmwood's new resident had for the French. Political activists harassed Gerry's family of females by constructing a guillotine in the field before his daughter's window, smearing it with blood, and attaching the effigy of a headless man. The poor women were terrified.

After Gerry gave up his mission in France and returned to Cambridge, local passions subsided. He ran unsuccessfully for Governor, then won two close elections in 1810 and 1811. During his second term in the State House, a law was passed redrawing the boundaries of the Commonwealth's senatorial districts so as to isolate Federalist districts and ensure more Republican victories in future elections. One of the newly created districts, in Essex County, looked rather like a salamander and gave birth to the expression "gerrymandering" though Gerry was not really responsible for fiddling with the boundary lines. Gerry was elected Madison's Vice President in 1812, but he expired before his term did. This was as close as any Cantabrigian has come to the office of U.S. President—excluding, of course, Harvard College graduates whose claims to Cambridge are even more tenuous than Gerry's, namely Presidents John Adams, Harvard 1755; John Quincy Adams, 1787; Theodore Roosevelt, 1880; Franklin D. Roosevelt, 1904; and John F. Kennedy, 1940. Gerry's widow in 1818 sold Elmwood to the Reverend Charles Lowell, pastor of the West Street Congregational Church in Boston. James Russell Lowell was born there the following year.

The John Vassall House, which Washington had used for his headquarters, had been bought in 1781 by a Newburyport shipowner named Nathaniel Tracy. Tracy was briefly but beautifully rich, and at the time he arrived in Cambridge he owned so many estates that it was rumored he could travel from Newburyport to Philadelphia and sleep every night in his own house. During his tenure the Vassall house witnessed one of the more bizarre scenes in its history. Tracy entertained Admiral d'Estaing (Count Jean Baptiste Charles Henri Hector, ancestor of French President Valéry Giscard d'Estaing) and a party of Frenchmen. Wishing to honor them properly, he served frog soup with a full-sized frog in each plate. And this in Cambridge, future home of Julia Child!

Tracy's collapsing financial balloon forced him to sell the Vassall estate to John Russell, who sold it to Andrew Craigie in 1793. Craigie had advanced considerably since the Battle of Bunker Hill. He had become the first Apothecary General of the United States and then dabbled profitably in various speculative enterprises. He occupied the Vassall mansion with his beautiful young wife, Elizabeth, and entertained in a style worthy of the former Tory occupants. Meanwhile he cast his shrewd speculator's eye on ways to augment his fortune.

B y 1788, the financial chaos and business depression which characterized the postwar period in America yielded to rising economic conditions. The economy grew energetically during the next two decades. Those who invested wisely made huge fortunes. Those who speculated foolishly lost their shirts. Cambridge men were not immune to temptation, and a number of them contracted the financial fever.

Unlike the old Tories who had made their money outside the town, many of the new economic aristocracy looked for investment opportunities right in Cambridge. Actually, there was little in the village's growth to generate economic optimism. The 1,600 or so inhabitants of 1775 had increased undramatically to 2,115 by

ENTER THE SPECULATORS

Cambridge's most glamorous historic site. Modern picture of the Vassall-Craigie-Longfellow House on Brattle Street. Here John Vassall, Jr., staged elaborate parties; George Washington planned his campaign against the British in Boston; Andrew Craigie engineered the development of Lechmere's Point; and Henry Wadsworth Longfellow produced some of the most enduring of American poetry. The estate now is the Longfellow National Historic Site, and the National Park Service maintains it as a museum. For its location see No. 3 in the map of Tory Row on page 21.

1790 (Cambridge then still included Arlington and Brighton). According to the Reverend Abiel Holmes's *History,* in 1793 there were only 148 houses in the village near the Common and in those days only four houses lay east of Dana Hill, which is a few blocks east of Harvard Yard. Cambridge by itself was not commercially inspiring. But no sophisticated imagination was required to grasp the inherent advantages of Cambridge's proximity to Boston and its value as a link between Boston and points north and west. The most obvious means of exploiting these assets was to build bridges—which is exactly what Cambridge speculators set out to do.

Andrew Cabot, the temporary owner of Elmwood, filed a petition for a bridge between Boston and Lechmere's Point, but the General Court denied the application in 1785—as, indeed, it had been denying such petitions since 1738. It is not at all clear why the General Court had turned down earlier bridge petitions and isolated the Boston peninsula for so long. Anyhow, this policy finally came to an end in 1785, the very year of Cabot's disappointment, when the Court approved a bridge between Boston and Charlestown—first proposed in 1720! The new Charles River Bridge, a toll bridge, opened in 1786 on the eleventh anniversary of the Battle of Bunker Hill amidst the thunder of cannons. It was an immediate financial success.

Cabot's failure did not diminish the enthusiasm for bridge building in Cambridge. Encouraged by the economic results of the Charlestown bridge, Judge Francis Dana soon led a new campaign for a Cambridge bridge. In the past Lechmere's Point had seemed the logical place, but the building of a fort on Dana Hill during the siege of Boston had alerted people to the possibilities of locating a bridge farther upriver than the Point, or a little closer to the Village. With this in mind, Dana organized other profit-minded businessmen and, in January 1792, the group opened a public subscription for 200 shares in a proposed West Boston Bridge; the shares sold in three hours. Dana and his associates filed their petition with the General Court in March.

Connections in high places are always helpful at a time like that, and Dana's personal friendship with Governor John Hancock undoubtedly speeded the project. The Court approved the petition quickly with the proviso that Harvard be paid £200 a year from the tolls. Construction began at once. The £200 a year to Harvard can be explained as follows. Harvard was only then beginning to recover from a financial mess incurred during the war because of currency inflation and the absent-minded bookkeeping of John Hancock, who had been college treasurer during the early years of the Revolution. The Commonwealth was helping to bail Harvard out.

The West Boston Bridge, on the site of the current Longfellow Bridge, measured 3,483 feet, more than twice the length of the Charlestown bridge. Besides, a 3,344-foot causeway spanned the marshes and mudflats on the Cambridge bank of the Charles. This impressive structure opened on November 23, 1793. People responded enthusiastically. They praised the elegance of the bridge's woodwork and the two rows of lamps which lighted it at night. "We hope," said the *Columbian Centinel,* "the Proprietors will not suffer pecuniary loss from their public spirit." Loss was not part of the shareholders' plan. Though the bridge had cost them £23,000, they fully expected to profit from their investment by the collection of tolls. Sample tolls: Foot passenger, 2/3 penny. One person and horse, 2-2/3 penny. Coaches, 1 shilling. Cattle, 1-1/3 penny each. "DOUBLE TOLL SHALL BE PAID ON THE LORD'S DAY." Despite the tolls, most travelers preferred the new convenient route to riding many miles through the countryside to the old Great Bridge and crossing toll-free. The proprietors made out well even after paying the £200 per year to Harvard which the Court had ordered. (The finances of the bridge were stated in pounds, shilling, and pence because, although the country went on the decimal system in 1792, the year the U.S. Mint was established at Philadelphia, it took some time for Americans to adjust to the new way of counting.)

The West Boston Bridge brought the first drastic alteration in Cambridge's

ENTER THE SPECULATORS

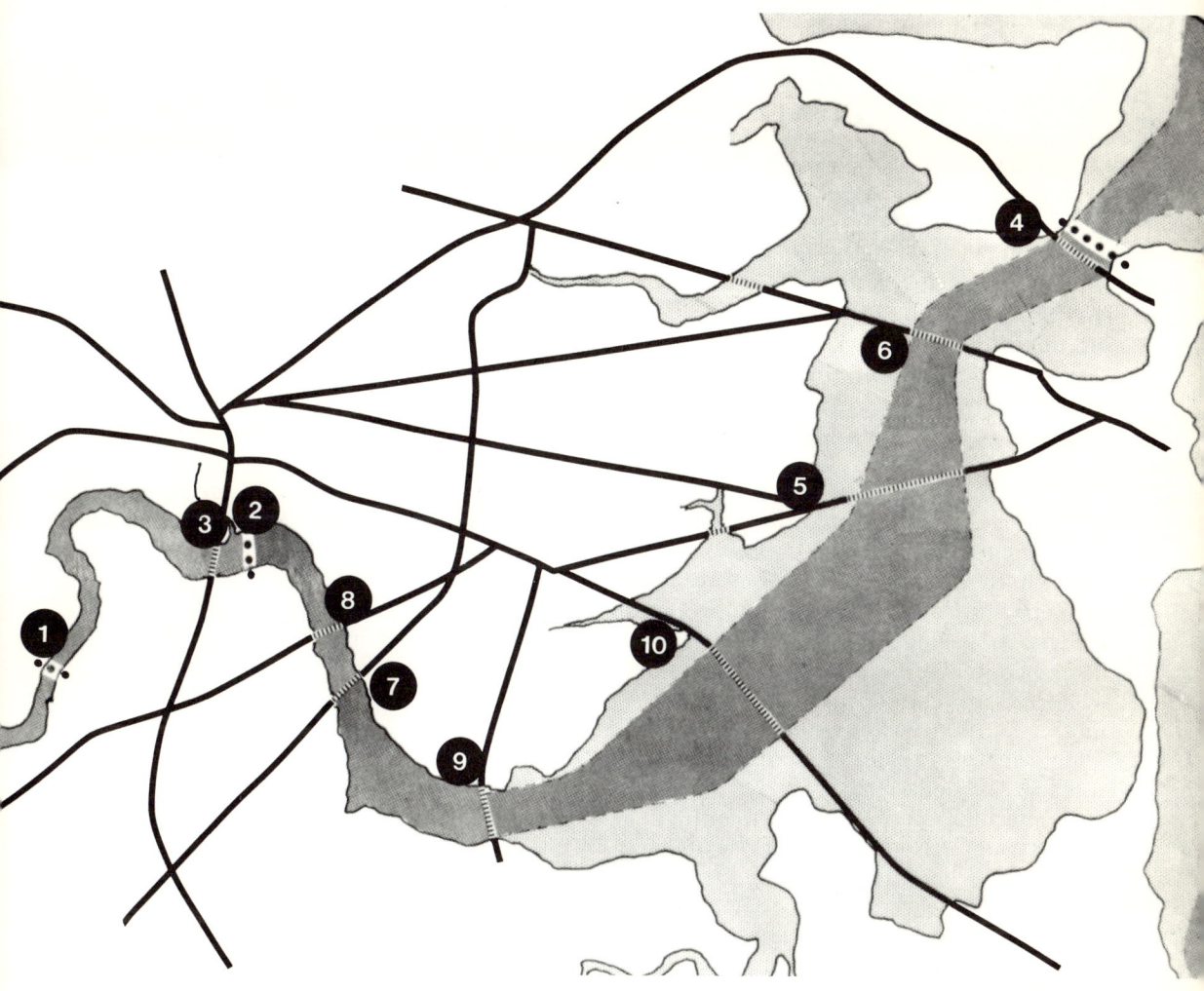

Charles River bridges to the end of the nineteenth century, as mapped by the Cambridge Historical Commission. Dark shading shows the water as it is now. Lighter shading shows it in the old days before the bay and the tidal marshes were filled in. The Boston peninsula is at the right.

1 and 2. Seventeenth-century ferries.
3. Great Bridge (at Old Cambridge), 1662.
4. Charles River Bridge (between Boston and Charlestown), 1786.
5. West Boston Bridge, 1793.
6. Canal (Craigie) Bridge, 1809.
7. River Street Bridge, 1810.
8. Western Avenue Bridge, 1824.
9. Brookline (Cottage Farm) Bridge, 1850.
10. Harvard Bridge (Massachusetts Avenue), 1890.

physiognomy since the founding of the town in 1630. First of all, it reduced the distance between the Cambridge Common and Boston from eight miles to around three and brought the agricultural interior of Middlesex County that much closer to its principal market. More important, as Wendell Garrett observed in "The Topographical Development of Cambridge" (*Proceedings of the Cambridge Historical Society,* 1961-1963), the town, which had been oriented inland, turned for the first time toward the river and the looming metropolis on the sea in symbolic acknowledgment that Cambridge's future growth depended on Boston.

The proprietors of the West Boston Bridge had not overlooked the probability that the new route would increase land values in the vicinity of the causeway. That property and most of what is now Cambridgeport belonged almost exclusively to three people. One was Andrew Bordman, who had inherited his land from his mother. Another was Leonard Jarvis, who bought the old Inman estate in 1792. The third was Judge Dana, who, by purchase and inheritance, owned more than half of Cambridgeport south of the present Massachusetts Avenue as well as sizable tracts to the north. After the bridge opened, Dana and Jarvis laid out building lots for houses and stores at the west end of the causeway. The first takers were Robert Vose and a young fellow heroically named Royal Makepeace. They opened a grocery store in December 1793. During the next year, Jarvis built a tavern on an adjacent lot, and before long there were more than half a dozen stores and houses in the neighborhood. Things were going beautifully for Dana and Jarvis, and they decided to upgrade the properties by draining some of the salt marshes and laying out new streets.

Suddenly, in 1798, everything came to a halt. Jarvis was in debt to the federal government in the amount of $40,000, which he failed to repay. The government seized his Cambridgeport lands and withdrew them from the market. All Cambridge was stunned. Jarvis was an elusive character; he had materialized in Cambridge in 1792, and he vanished under fire in 1798.

No one, presumably including the good Judge Dana, seems to have known much about him or how he got into his personal financial mess, but he had speculated with the recklessness of a riverboat gambler, probably taking short-term loans to finance long-term projects. As far as the development of the lands by the causeway went, however, Jarvis's disaster proved a blessing. The government divided his estate into fifty-four lots and sold them at public auction in 1801. This evidence of public interest convinced Andrew Bordman of the wisdom of dividing and selling his property, too.

Among the eager buyers of Cambridgeport land were the enterprising Robert Vose and Royal Makepeace. From the vantage point of their grocery store, they determined to share in the profit-taking that was occurring beneath their noses. Vose died in 1803, and Makepeace found a new partner for the store. In his real estate ventures, he associated with Rufus Davenport, an ambitious Boston merchant. The peculiar idea of creating "Cambridgeport," a real port on the Cambridge waterfront, sprang from the fertile imaginations of these two men. A good port complete with docking facilities already existed in Boston, whereas the waters of the Charles were shallow and the dangers of running aground considerable. But Makepeace and Davenport rushed into their adventure. They projected a network of canals for the loading and unloading of cargoes. In retrospect, James Russell Lowell wrote unsympathetically, "The marshes were bought, canals were dug ample for the commerce of both Indies, and four or five rows of brick houses were built to meet the first wants of the wading settlers who were expected to rush in WHENCE?"

The first Cambridgeport settlement was in the vicinity of the present Kendall Square, though one would never surmise such humble antecedents from the modern towers which stand there today. Congress certified Cambridge a port of entry on January 11, 1805. Stores, taverns, and houses were already springing up along new roads. These included Concord Street, now Broadway; extension of the Middlesex

ENTER THE SPECULATORS

Cambridgeport scene. This is Lafayette Square (junction of Main Street and Massachusetts Avenue) in the middle 1820s. Hovey Tavern is at left, and the First Universalist Church is the white building at the right beyond a tree.

Turnpike, now Hampshire Street; and the "Road from Colleges to the West Boston bridge," now Massachusetts Avenue and Main Street. More tradesmen moved into the neighborhood, and wharves were built along the canals. Drained marshes were filled with gravel, and gardens were planted here and there. To accommodate the growing population the town of Cambridge built a school house in Cambridgeport in 1802. A fire society, equipped with a first-rate engine, was formed in 1803. By 1806 over a thousand people lived in the Cambridgeport settlement. On January 1, 1807, a capacious brick meeting house, the First Cambridgeport Church, was dedicated on Columbia Street.

Cambridge never had a fighting chance to prove itself a port. The canal network was scarcely completed before Congress, on President Jefferson's recommendation, passed the first trade embargo act in response to British and French trade restrictions. The legislation, approved by representatives of southern and western states over the strenuous objections of the northern shipping states, prohibited further commerce with foreign countries. It was voted near the end of 1807. All New England was in an uproar, and Cambridgeport speculators panicked. Makepeace, Dana, and Judge Samuel Fay, an active Cantabrigian who lived over by the Common, wrote the president pleading for a suspension of the embargo at least in reference to Spain, Portugal, and their South American colonies. Jefferson responded lengthily with reasons why he could not satisfy the inhabitants of Cambridge.

The embargo threw the development of Cambridgeport into reverse. Just as it had expanded on promises and hopes, it contracted at the first threat to aspirations. The absence of ships at the new wharves hurt less than the general regional business paralysis which the embargo produced, for ships had never been numerous there anyhow. Cambridgeport speculators hurried to dump property upon a listless market. Land which had formerly sold for 20 cents a square foot went for less than a penny. Money was tight, and no one was willing to build new houses or stores. Rufus Davenport and some associates, perhaps hoping to stimulate a revival of prosperity, went through the motions of incorporating the "Cambridgeport manufactory" in 1809, ostensibly to produce salt and cotton cloth. This establishment further announced plans to make printing types in 1813—by which time Cambridgeport had hit rock bottom. But, since the tenacious historian Lucius Paige found no physical traces of the factory, it is safe to assume that it existed only on paper.

During the first spurt of activity at the port, Andrew Craigie, dean of all Cambridge speculators, sat quietly at the Vassall mansion hatching his own plan. He had borrowed Andrew Cabot's old dream of a bridge between Lechmere's Point and Boston, and he proceeded to realize it with elaborate skill. In 1795 he began a series of surreptitious acquisitions of estates out on the Point. Those who believe that business intrigue and dummy corporations are contemporary phenomena should study Craigie's manipulations of Lechmere's Point real estate for a glimpse of a Great American Tradition. In one of those transactions, Craigie set up the sale of Andrew Cabot's lands (the old Lechmere estate plus part of the Phips farm) to Seth Johnson of New York, who mortgaged it to John Cabot. Two years later Johnson, for a nominal fee, turned over his interest in the land to Bossenger Foster, who just happened to be Craigie's brother-in-law. A decorous six months elapsed before Foster conveyed the estate to Craigie. Deals such as this one concealed the fact that one person was acquiring a tremendous amount of land and prevented the development of a speculative stampede.

Though Craigie's relatives acquired title to various lands in round-about fashion, not one deed was registered in Andrew Craigie's name before 1803, by which time he had just about accomplished his first objective. As nearly as anyone can tell, he paid less than $20,000 for 300 acres of land extending from the Point to beyond the present Inman Square. With land selling for 20 cents a foot over in Cambridgeport, and with Jarvis, Makepeace, and Davenport on the loose, it is easy to see why Craigie kept his plans secret.

Craigie now formed a corporation, which applied for the General Court's sanction to erect a bridge between Leverett Street in Boston and the east end of Lechmere's Point—on the site of the present Charles River Dam. Permission was granted in 1807. The prospect of the bridge instantly increased the value of Craigie's properties. Setting aside sufficient land for construction of the bridge and access routes, he divided the balance into sixty shares which he put on the market at $6,000 each. Eight shares sold immediately, and Craigie had already more than doubled his original investment. No doubt he would have done even better had not buyers been cautious during the embargo.

Meanwhile Craigie had headaches. Cambridge had decided to lay out a new road originating at Elmwood, then Elbridge Gerry's residence. The Cambridgeport proprietors backed a course

ENTER THE SPECULATORS

from Elmwood to the present Brattle Square, whereas Craigie wanted the road to run in a straight line to the present junction of Brattle and Mason Streets, near the Cambridge Common. The first route would lead straight toward Cambridgeport and the West Boston Bridge, the second toward Lechmere's Point and Craigie's bridge. The town changed its mind twice and then settled on the first route, much to Craigie's annoyance. The road now is called Mount Auburn Street.

The Canal Bridge, a toll bridge, opened on August 30, 1809—commencement day at Harvard. There was a great procession, led by Craigie in his coach and including the Governor, Harvard's president, and many notables. Somewhat less magnificent than the West Boston Bridge, it measured only 2,800 feet, but, like its predecessor, it twinkled prettily with lamps at night. Craigie's bridge, like the West Boston Bridge, paid off handsomely. By the time the two bridges became free in 1858, the successive owners had collected more than $2 million in tolls.

Craigie's next move was to form a real estate and development corporation to dispose of the shareholders' land to the general public. The "Lechmere Point Corporation" laid out Cambridge Street to make the connection between Old Cambridge and the new bridge. This new road, including a causeway through marshlands, constituted the first solid ground between the Point and the Cambridge "mainland." The corporation further engaged Peter Tufts, a Cambridgeport surveyor, to devise a street and lot plan, which he did by imposing a simple grid on the highlands with scant regard for the marginal marshes and flats. Looking at his work, one is reminded of Frederick Law Olmsted's comment that the grid form "was hit upon by the chance occurrence of a mason's sieve near a map of the ground to be laid out. It was taken up and placed upon the map, and the question being asked 'what do you want better than that?' no one was able to answer."

Craigie and his partners were interested in quick profits, not in topographical embellishments. Unfortunately for them, business started sluggishly. Only ten lots had been sold by mid-1813. Craigie, aware of the Cambridgeport doldrums, determined to rescue his own venture and applied the full force of his promotional genius to the problem. First he succeeded in convincing the Boston Porcelain and Glass Company to move out to the Point. Second—and Craigie's real coup—he brought about the removal of the Middlesex County courthouse and jail from Old Cambridge. This he accomplished by offering, on behalf of his corporation, to donate land and build thereon at a cost of $24,000 a new courthouse and jail to replace the overcrowded and dilapidated facilities near the College. Old Cambridge protested. Cambridgeport promoters protested vigorously. But the General Court approved the plan. A monumental courthouse and a smaller jail, both presumably designed by Charles Bulfinch—and if not by him, by an architect who imitated his style expertly—rose on the Point between 1814 and 1816. The courthouse, much altered, still stands on Third Street in East Cambridge.

The capture of the county buildings assured the success of the Lechmere Point Corporation. From that time on, building lots sold briskly. In the long run, however, and beyond the vision of the speculators, the modest little glass factory did more to determine the character of East Cambridge than the splendid courthouse.

Andrew Craigie had maneuvered through these dealings with the agility of a matador in the presence of an ornery bull. His story ends back in Old Cambridge. Somehow he lost control over his many speculative enterprises. He died in 1819 leaving a vast estate hopelessly encumbered by debts. His widow reduced the number of servants from twelve to two and rented out rooms in the once glorious Vassall House in order to pay the bills. Her most famous lodger was the poet Henry Wadsworth Longfellow. When Longfellow married Frances Appleton in 1843, her father, Nathan, purchased the house and presented it to him, and so it is generally known by his name, as "Longfellow House."

Middlesex County Courthouse in East Cambridge as it appeared in 1848. The original building, believed to have been designed by Charles Bulfinch, was begun in 1814. Ammi B. Young, architect of Boston's well-known Customs House, enlarged it in 1848.

5

Reluctant City

Just as things were getting underway down at the Port and out at the Point, the General Court of Massachusetts trimmed Cambridge boundaries again. West Cambridge (Arlington) and Brighton were set off in 1807. This left the old village with its college, the struggling Port, and the incipient development on Lechmere's Point—three areas separated by undeveloped lands and conflicting interests. Old Cambridge, Cambridgeport, and East Cambridge immediately started to act as if they were surrounded by mutually antagonistic magnetic fields. It was the pattern of growth, rather than the fact of growth, which determined the dynamics of the rivalries. If the town had grown around the traditional center of the Common and crawled out towards the river and the Point, the causes for quarrel might have come to the surface more slowly. This does not necessarily mean that Cambridge would have fewer problems today—only different ones.

Instead the character of Cambridge political life developed with a kind of inevitability. The two new settlements fought scrappily for anything they could get while the old village tried to hang on to what it had. Anyone looking at a map could have mistaken Cambridge for three villages, and a visitor to a town meeting would have watched a three-way tug-of-war. The trouble began even before the Canal Bridge was built, when Craigie squabbled with the West Boston Bridge proprietors over the course of Mount Auburn Street. Cambridgeport and East Cambridge promoters competed like Macy's and Gimbels during a price war. They vied for traffic over the bridges and they argued about roads and rights-of-way. They never entertained the notion of cooperation because cooperation did not mix with profit. They built streets through Old Cambridge and on to the north, but it was decades before a direct route connected the Port with the Point.

As long as the speculators did not meddle with the west end of town, Old Cambridge viewed the changes with satisfaction or, in the case of the port scheme, bewilderment. The residents were delighted with the new bridges, which abbreviated their trips to Boston. People with commercial interests were enthusiastic. Only seven years after the opening of the West Boston Bridge, the Rev. Abiel Holmes, father of one Oliver Wendell Holmes and grandfather of another, wrote that "the erection of the bridge has very perceptibly influenced the trade of Cambridge, which was formerly very inconsiderable. By bringing the travel from the westward and northward through the town it has greatly invigorated business there." There were some furrowed brows and mutterings over the rowdy activities down in the taverns along the Port waterfront, but if Cambridge had survived the Continental Army it could tolerate a few drunken wagon drivers down by the river.

This benign attitude reversed itself abruptly on the day when Old Cambridge discovered the Lechmere Point Corporation trying to make off with the county courthouse and jail. No one debated the inadequacies of the existing buildings at Harvard Square; they had been overstuffed for years. And here came Andrew Craigie, all smiles and generosity, offering to donate brand-new facilities—in East Cambridge. Old Cambridge cried foul, and the gift was refused. The real issue was not the complaint most often cited—the nuisance of traveling out to the Point to conduct business with the courts—but the loss of prestige for Old Cambridge. When the Massachusetts General Court forced them to accept Craigie's charity, many Cantabrigians felt as though a surgeon had excised some vital organ from the civic body and transplanted it to an alien host. No matter what the maps said about town boundaries, Old Cambridge did not consider the Point

CAMBRIDGE RECONSIDERED

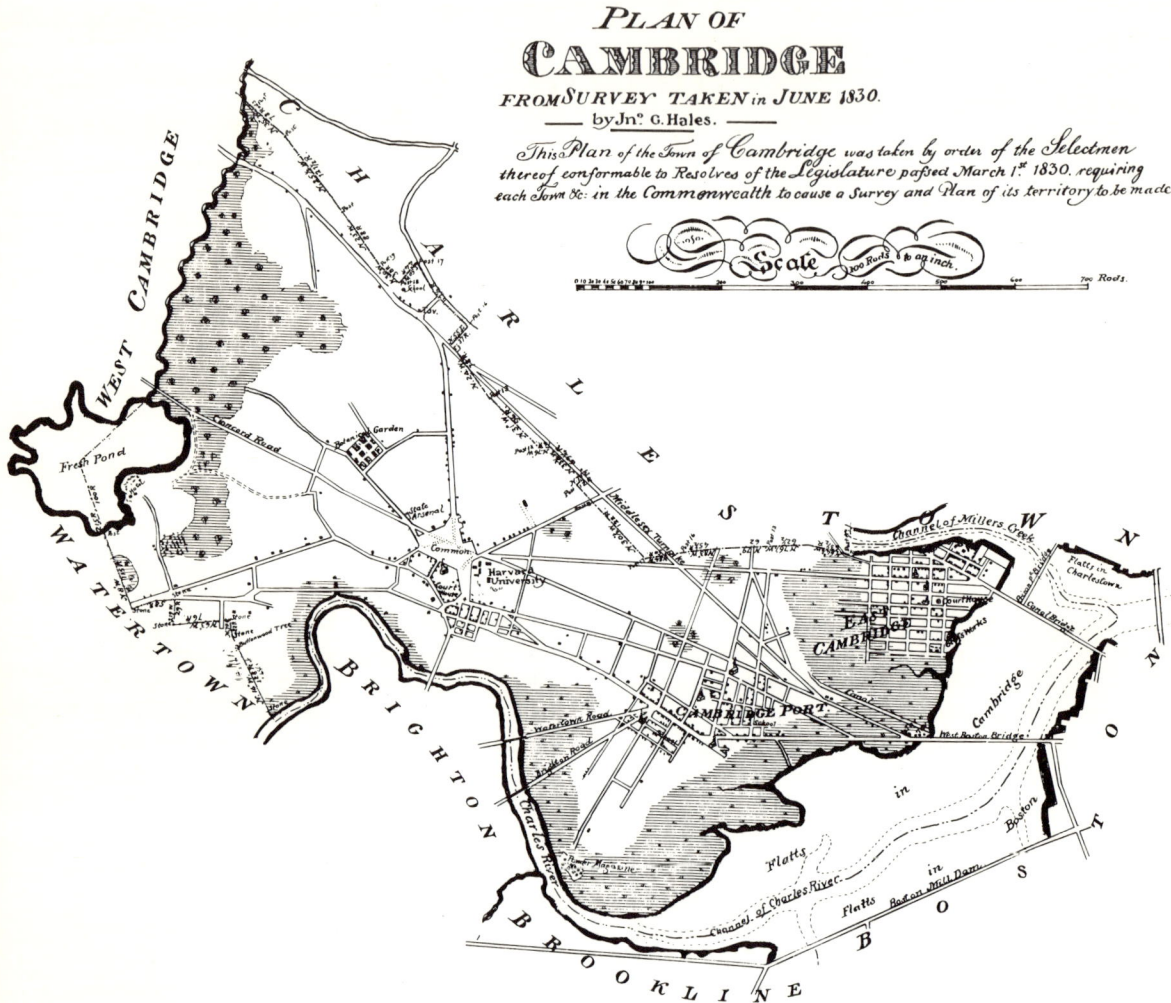

Cambridge in 1830, based on a survey made in June of that year by John G. Hales. The three lines of script under the title say that the Selectmen had ordered the plan to be made in accordance with a Massachusetts act of March 1. Notice the word "Charlestown" all across top of plan; most of that territory now is in Somerville. "West Cambridge," which had been detached from Cambridge in 1807, now is called Arlington. Old Cambridge, containing Harvard, is near center of map, and the waffle-like site to its northwest is the Botanical Garden. To right of Old Cambridge is Cambridgeport, with its West Boston Bridge; and farther right is East Cambridge, with its Canal Bridge. Shaded areas at left end of map are fresh-water lowlands, and those along the river are salt marshes. The river channel at low tide is shown by dotted lines.

or the Port authentic Cambridge. The distinctions still linger. People who live in the Harvard neighborhood describe themselves as residents of "Cambridge," whereas others often locate themselves in North Cambridge, East Cambridge, Riverside, or some other area.

After Craigie ran off with the courthouse, Old Cambridge folk woke up to the seriousness of the new villages within their town. Cambridgeport already had its own meeting house and school house, and East Cambridge grew around the county buildings and industry. Instead of looking toward Old Cambridge as the source of power, the new areas generated centers of their own. Furthermore, it had become apparent in the courthouse transaction that the new settlements did not respect the sanctity of the old. Old Cambridge took steps to defend itself against further abuses.

In 1823 the town meeting received a proposal from some Old Cambridge individuals to grade the Common, plant trees and shrubs, and put a fence around it— entirely at their own expense. The Selectmen shunted the petition off to a committee where it appeared to have died. However, activity continued behind the scenes, and seven years later the General Court authorized the small contingent of private citizens to carry out their plan. East Cambridge businessmen did not approve, for it eliminated the direct connection between Cambridge Street and the Concord Turnpike and also between Cambridge Street and Brattle Street via Mason Street. Out-of-town cattle drivers were also displeased since they were accustomed to using the Common as a resting place for their stock en route to Boston. Thus the enclosure of the Common became a hot political issue.

So many people turned out for the town meeting on October 8, 1830, that they were forced to adjourn from the old courthouse (which had become the customary assembly place) to the fourth meeting house. An ill-tempered debate ensued, and the town voted 169 to 119 in favor of enclosing the Common. This was probably the first town meeting where the vote reflected clear regional divisions. Subsequent efforts

Cambridge Common in the 1970s. Weather like this — not unusual in Cambridge — no doubt made life uncomfortable for the Continental Army troops quartered here two centuries ago. The Common had roads through it until it was enclosed in 1830.

by the opponents of enclosure to repeal the legislature's authorization and to petition for a highway across the Common failed, and Old Cambridge won its battle.

But the quarrel had been fierce, and some ungodly language had shaken the meeting house rafters. If town meetings were going to be verbal brawls—and all signs pointed in that direction—the members of the parish questioned the propriety of staging them in their place of worship. The need for a new hall for town meetings was obvious. The Selectmen hastily designated a committee, consisting of three members from each section of Cambridge, to consider an appropriate location. For a change, East Cambridge and Cambridgeport found a common cause and lined up against Old Cambridge. The committee determined on a site in Cambridgeport, on the corner of Harvard and Norfolk streets. This choice demonstrated sound geographic logic, for the new town house inconvenienced almost everybody equally and therefore might be considered the most democratic solution. The building opened in March 1832. Old Cambridge had surrendered its last symbol of civic power.

This chronicle of rough political turmoil, though crucial to the understanding of today's city, obscures the softer and more amusing aspects of ordinary life in Cambridge. This divided, quarrelsome Cambridge was also the playground of James Russell Lowell's boyhood. In 1854 the poet and professor, in his *Fireside Travels,* described the Cambridge of 1824 as "a country village with its own habits and traditions, not yet feeling too strongly the force of suburban gravitation." Lowell continued: "Approaching it from the west, by what was then called the New Road [Mount Auburn Street], you would pause on the brow of Symond's Hill [at Channing Street] to enjoy a view singularly soothing and placid. In front of you lay the town, tufted with elms, lindens and horse-chestnuts, which had seen Massachusetts a colony, and were fortunately unable to emigrate with Tories, by whom, or by whose fathers, they were planted. Over it rose the noisy belfry of the College, the square, brown tower of the Episcopal Church, and the slim, yellow spire of the parish meeting-house. To your left upon the Old Road [Brattle Street] you saw some half-dozen dignified old houses of the colonial time."

"We called it 'The Village' then," wrote Lowell, "and it was essentially an English village—quiet, unspeculative, without enterprise, sufficing to itself, and only showing such differences from the original types as the public school and the system of town government might superinduce. A few houses, chiefly old, stood around the bare common, with ample elbow-room; and old women, capped and spectacled, still peered through the same windows from which they had watched Lord Percy's artillery rumble by to Lexington, or caught a glimpse of the handsome Virginia general who had come to wield our homespun Saxon chivalry. The hooks were to be seen from which had swung the hammocks of Burgoyne's captive red-coats. If memory does not deceive me, women still washed clothes in the town spring [near the corner of Eliot and Brattle streets] clear as that of Bandalusia." Lowell added that one coach sufficed for all the travel to Boston.

Such reminiscences sifted down through Cambridge history from the upper social stratum most likely to produce fond images. From Lowell, living grandly at Elmwood. From the Autocrat of the Breakfast Table, Oliver Wendell Holmes, poet and physician, who grew up comfortably in what he called an "honest mansion," where Harvard's Austin Hall was later built, "not one of those Tory Episcopal-church-goers strongholds." Or from Thomas Wentworth Higginson, who was born in the first house on Professor's Row (Kirkland Street). These men all looked back mistily upon the village of their youth. They were literary men before social realism came into vogue.

But Old Cambridge was 200 years old in 1830, and many of its buildings were decrepit. It was no longer an agricultural town; the serious farmers had deserted it for the richer, open lands of the American midwest. Besides Harvard faculty members, most of the villagers were artisans, tradesmen, gardeners, servants, or liverymen. They lived in poorly lit houses, many of which had declined from single-family dwellings to stores and tenements. Aside from a few small vegetable gardens, people no longer cultivated their own food. A wooden market building was erected in the middle of the present Harvard Square in 1812, and there it stood until 1833 emitting powerful fragrances on hot summer afternoons. Old Cambridge streets, like those of most cities, turned to mud in rainstorms, and there was no sewage system or garbage collection. No doubt "the Village" was picturesque, but not everyone could view it as affectionately as Lowell.

Now that the county buildings were in East Cambridge and the town hall in Cambridgeport, Harvard reigned unchallenged in Old Cambridge. The college's land holdings had trebled since the Revolution, and

buildings multiplied in Harvard Yard. There was the new Stoughton Hall, designed by Charles Bulfinch and built in 1804; Holworthy Hall (1811); University Hall (1813, more Bulfinch); Dane Hall (1832); and Gore Hall (1838), a Gothic monstrosity which most people loved. Divinity Hall, built in 1825, was the first major Harvard building outside the Yard. Harvard had a medical school, founded in 1783, and a law school, founded in 1817. It was officially a university, but the term "Harvard University" was slow to come into use. Instead, the documents of the time usually referred to the whole institution as "Harvard College" or "the University in Cambridge"—even sometimes "the University *of* Cambridge." Indeed, even now the legal name of the Harvard Corporation is not Harvard University but "President and Fellows of Harvard College."

Apparently no one saw anything sinis-

A pastoral scene in Harvard Square, 1830.
The artist was looking southward from the Common. The Fourth Meeting House stands in the college yard at the left. It was built in 1756 and survived until 1833. It was used for worship, town meetings, and college ceremonies. Here the town fashioned petitions stating its grievances against the British; here the Massachusetts constitution was framed in 1780; and here in 1830 the town voted to enclose the Common. The small building beneath the trees, right of center, was a market building which was removed a few years later.

ter in Harvard's growth or complained about the acquisition of real estate. Cambridge still had undeveloped land to spare. The popular John T. Kirkland—a "jolly little man," according to Longfellow—presided over the college from 1810 to 1828. The absent-minded but undeniably capable Josiah Quincy, a former Boston mayor, replaced Kirkland and oversaw the celebration of Harvard's bicentennial in 1836—140 years before that of the United States.

This was the period when Old Cambridge acquired the academic luster which still characterizes it. With the Tories gone and the speculators on the wane, Harvard personalities became the new Cambridge luminaries. The lavish entertainments of Phipses, Vassalls, and Craigies gave way to the more bookish activities of the scholarly elite. Cambridge society was more impressed by learning than by big bank accounts. The real money lived over in Boston and sent its sons to Harvard. Generations of Harvard professors became famous for their intellectual achievements, their wit, and their idiosyncrasies.

For instance, Old Cambridge could gossip about Dr. Benjamin Waterhouse, who established the practice of smallpox vaccination in the United States. In 1800 he inoculated four Cambridge people with cowpox, which had been introduced by Edward Jenner in England. The process was so feared that Waterhouse was blamed for a serious smallpox epidemic until a Boston committee of health investigators pronounced that the cow vaccine was indeed an effective preventative. Waterhouse wrote a tract on the evils of tobacco, laid out the college botanical garden, and taught at the medical school until 1812 when he took an unpopular stand on an administrative (not scientific) issue and was forced to resign. But he liked Cambridge and continued to live there in his house north of the Common on the street which now carries his name. He made other important medical discoveries. He also stalked Cambridge streets providing grist for Lowell's literary mill: "I remember he used to turn his whole person in order to bring the foci of his great spectacles to bear upon any object. One can fancy that terrified Nature would have yielded up her secrets at once, without cross-examination, at their first glare."

The Reverend Charles Follen lived on Waterhouse Street from 1830 to 1835. He taught German at Harvard and may have introduced the first Christmas tree to the United States. Joseph Story, Associate Justice of the U.S. Supreme Court, first Dane Professor of Law at Harvard, lived on the corner of what are now Story and Brattle Streets. He was a colossal presence, both in the law school and in Cambridge society. He participated actively in municipal affairs—at least in those that concerned him—and was the single most influential person in winning the right to enclose the Common. In 1837 a youthful Longfellow walked up the path to the Vassall House and asked the widow Craigie to rent him rooms. "Young man, I do not take undergraduates," replied this once beautiful woman who had lived in splendor. She relented when Longfellow succeeded in convincing her that he was a professor, not a student, and the poet moved in as a boarder, never dreaming that he would eventually own the house. Ralph Waldo Emerson lived out in Concord but was no stranger in Cambridge. He delivered the Phi Beta Kappa address at Harvard in 1837 and spoke about "The American Scholar," calling for American intellectual independence from Europe. This was rarefied Cambridge—the stuff that created the Cambridge legend.

The irrepressible Professor Lowell wrote not only about the 1824 "village" but also about 1824 Cambridgeport. Most of it, he said, was a "huckleberry pastur." "Its veins did not draw their blood from the quiet old heart of the village, but it had a distinct being of its own, and was rather a great caravansary than a suburb. The chief feature of the place was its inns, of which there were five, with vast barns and court-yards . . . There were, besides the taverns, some huge square stores where groceries were sold, some houses, by whom or why inhabited was to us boys a problem, and, on the edge of the marsh, a currier's shop, where, at high tide, on a floating platform, men were always beating skins in a way to remind one of Don Quixote's fulling mills."

Actually, Cambridgeport in the 1820s was still in economic trouble. Though the trade embargo had ended in 1815, the new settlement recovered its former energy very slowly. There was no enthusiasm for reviving the port, which had been idle since 1807. The wharves were rotting, silt had collected in the canals, and confidence in the venture had evaporated. Prospective buyers heard too many woeful financial tales and shied away. Makepeace and Davenport gradually went bankrupt. Judge Dana's heirs, however, shrewdly held on to their massive real estate holdings until the 1830s when the economic picture began to improve.

The two speculative interests in Cambridgeport had worked at cross purposes. Davenport and Makepeace had invested mainly in fantasy while the proprietors of the West Boston Bridge stuck stubbornly with the more pedestrian, but more realistic, premise of capitalizing on the nearness of Boston. Thus, while the former dug their financial graves with the port, the proprietors quietly built the River Street Bridge in 1810 in order to open up the lands south of the present Massachusetts Avenue. The port debacle and the embargo delayed quick profits; nevertheless, by the early 1820s there were streets and houses in the area. Encouraged, the proprietors then built the Western Avenue Bridge in 1824. Thus a second district was settled at some distance upriver from the original Cambridgeport community near the port and canals. The three bridge arteries converged at the haymarket, now Central Square, joined, and proceeded through the mile or so of woods, brush, and pastureland to Old Cambridge. The removal of the town hall to Cambridgeport vastly improved financial prospects there and prompted the Danas to divide and sell their land; this gave a great stimulus to settlement.

The specter of the port and its failure scared business investors for a number of years during which Cambridgeport's chief excuse for being was that it lay between the agricultural hinterlands and the Boston market. Gradually, however, small manufacturing made tentative beginnings. Livermore, Crane & Whitney, a soap factory founded in 1804, survived the embargo. A second soap factory appeared in 1828, a third in 1835, and a fourth in 1840, providing Cambridgeport with a small-scale, smelly industry. A confectioner arrived in 1826, Ebenezer Hovey opened a bacon-curing place in the 1840s, and George Page started making boxes in 1845. The biggest manufacturing concern belonged to Charles Davenport, whose firm made carriages and stagecoaches. It opened for business in 1832 in the present Central Square and later expanded into a large plant on Main Street farther east. These were mostly small operations, however, and Cambridgeport could not employ all the people who lived there.

Many Cambridgeport men crossed the Charles to work in Boston and returned in the evening to their detached, wood-frame, one-family or two-family houses. A typical inhabitant, perhaps, was the young Elias Howe, who had left his father's farm in Spencer, Massachusetts, and settled in the Port in 1837. Every day he went to Boston to his job with a watchmaker. Then he broke out of the typical mold. One day at work he overheard a conversation about a machine for sewing, and he became obsessed with the idea. By 1845 he had invented a machine with an eyed needle and a threading device which could fasten stitches at regular intervals in fabric. He had difficulty selling his contraption and would have needed an Andrew Craigie to advance it properly. A British corset-maker recognized its worth and imported Howe to develop the machine; he took advantage of Howe's innocence in business and exploited him. Even worse, when Howe returned to the United States in 1849, he discovered that Isaac Singer had violated his patent rights. The inventor sued and won royalties on all sewing machines sold in the United States until 1867.

"The Port must have had its attractions because so many wonderful people lived there," Dr. Oliver Wendell Holmes observed, though its attractions were beyond his imagination. Margaret Fuller,

Margaret Fuller (1810-1850), feminist, reformer, writer. She was born in Cambridgeport and spent her childhood there. She became associated with Ralph Waldo Emerson and the Concord literary circle. In her late thirties she married an Italian nobleman. With their infant son they were drowned in a shipwreck.

Washington Allston (1779-1843). This self-portrait was painted between 1801 and 1805. He was born in South Carolina and was in the Harvard class of 1800. Later he had his studio in Cambridgeport near the present Central Square. He was called the "American Titian." Courtesy of the Museum of Fine Arts, Boston.

feminist and later editor of the Transcendentalist review *Dial,* grew up in the Port. At fifteen she already knew Greek, French, Italian, and philosophy; she dazzled her elders with brilliant conversation. Washington Allston, a talented eccentric painter, worked in a bare wooden studio on the corner of Magazine and Auburn streets. Richard Henry Dana, grandson of old Judge Francis, grew up in Cambridgeport and wrote *Two Years before the Mast* there. Thomas Wentworth Higginson reported that the finest private library in all Cambridge belonged to Thomas Dowse, a leather dresser who lived in Cambridgeport.

That such people could reside in Cambridgeport caused some astonishment in Old Cambridge. The Port seemed such a rude, awkward, unrefined place. Higginson recalled his passages through it as unpleasant episodes. "When we went to Boston it was by taking 'Morse's hourly' [the stage] and passing through the then open region, past Dana Hill, to the 'Port,' where we sometimes had to encounter, even on the stage-box, the open irreverence of the 'Port chucks,' who kept up a local antagonism." He said the Port delegation "seemed to be larger and more pugnacious . . . than the sons of professors and college stewards."

Concerning *East* Cambridge in 1824, James Russell Lowell remained mute. The settlement out at Lechmere's Point had progressed with a more deliberate rhythm than Cambridgeport. Because there had been no early artificial inflation of population, there was no ruinous collapse. Craigie's bridge and Boston-oriented plan had been sound from the start. When land sales were slow, the Lechmere Point Corporation enticed buyers by promising that landholders would have free passage across the bridge. By 1818, East Cambridge had a school and a church organization; by 1825 the population had passed the one thousand mark. Spiritually it had a closer affinity with Boston across the bridge than with Old Cambridge.

Industry flowed more steadily into the Point than it did to the Port, possibly because there was no stigma of financial failure to frighten investors. When Boston Porcelain & Glass went under during the embargo, another firm leased its quarters, and in 1817 the New England Glass Company bought the place at public auction. They expanded the works and built a thriving industry. Under the energetic guidance of Deming Jarves, New England Glass was soon turning out $65,000 worth of merchandise a year—everything from plain glass to chandeliers for churches. A brush factory, a furniture company, and the largest soap factory in the United States were all out at the Point by 1840. In addition to local industries there were the commercial activities associated with the goods passing through to Boston. Farmers drove cattle, hogs, and turkeys down Cambridge Street and stopped at either of the two taverns, Mansion or Lechmere House, near the Canal Bridge.

Meanwhile the courthouse and jail perched nobly on Putnam Hill. Inside the jail, prisoners led a sordid existence, as Dorothea Dix discovered when she taught Sunday school classes there in 1841. The insane and common criminals were thrown together, regardless of age or sex. Prisoners were often unclothed in damp, cold cells; some were chained to walls and flogged. Dix, appropriately horrified, began her pioneering efforts at prison reform. Lawyers, clerks, officers, and prison authorities who served Middlesex County lived near the courthouse and constituted the Point's social upper crust. Factory workers had little Georgian cottages along Winter, Gore, Bridge, and Cambridge streets. Businessmen lived on Thorndike and Otis streets. Housing ranged from the simple cottages to elegant townhouses, and the atmosphere was congenial. Here, as in other parts of Cambridge, social distinctions caused few conflicts. Nearly all the inhabitants came from an Anglo-Saxon background, and one of the values they shared at that period was a profound respect for established hierarchy.

East Cambridge had a healthy balance of commerce, industry, and professionalism; no one activity dominated the others. The village at the Point was physically compact and geographically distinct from the rest of Cambridge. It grew neatly, according to the original plan. By the 1830s it had a second grammar school and four churches. By 1846 East Cambridge nurtured four thousand people.

Cambridge as a whole had increased its population from 2,323 in 1810 to 8,409 in 1840—a rate three times greater than that of the Commonwealth of Massachusetts. During the next five years Cambridge grew an astonishing 48 percent, and the 1845 population figure was 12,490. Most of the growth had occurred in Cambridgeport and East Cambridge, and most of the people who had settled there had abandoned farmlands in the western part of the state or moved over from Boston. The governing factor was migration, not a soaring birth rate. By 1845 the town of Cambridge had thirteen schools and seventeen churches. The tiny old buryingground near the Common had long passed the point of usefulness. Cambridgeport and East Cambridge now buried their dead in a cemetery between Broadway and Harvard streets, and Old Cambridge, after 1832, laid its fold to rest more grandly in Mount Auburn cemetery, America's first rural garden cemetery—nearly all of which lies across the Cambridge line in Watertown. Cambridge also had three post offices, one in each village.

As more roads and houses were built, the separate sections crept closer to one another without resolving their political difficulties. The distribution of public funds caused continual arguments. Cambridgeport and East Cambridge, though agreeing about little else, concurred that they did not receive a just proportion of public conveniences. They built their own roads, which everybody used, but also helped pay for street maintenance in Old Cambridge. They further suspected a reluctance on the part of Old Cambridge to approve their fair share of schools. Meanwhile, if either of the new sections won some battle, the other was usually jealous. Since no one part of the town could control the other two, expedient political alliances solidified and dissolved according to need. Whatever the decision, one part of town usually felt abused or neglected.

Many Old Cambridge residents had never forgiven the loss of the county buildings or the town hall. They observed the accumulating power of the nether regions with alarm and the commercial-industrial character of the new communities with distaste. If this was not a universal view, it was nevertheless the prevailing opinion among many Old Cambridge people. In December 1842, a number of them petitioned the Massachusetts legislature, the General Court, to set off Old Cambridge as a separate town—or rather, by their wording, to have Cambridgeport and East Cambridge set off from Old Cambridge. The suggestion shocked the town and caused a commotion. Representatives from *all* parts of Cambridge argued against the petition and, as the petitioners' most potent argument was the existence of three post offices, the General Court declined to act on the request. The Old Cambridge clique then brought the matter before the town meeting, where it was easily defeated in February 1846.

As often happens, the effort to do one thing achieved quite the opposite. The separation attempt frightened the Selectmen into administrative reorganization in the interest of a more efficient government. Following the examples of Boston, Salem, and Lowell, the town meeting then sought a more binding form of alliance by petitioning for a city charter.

The General Court granted the petition pending formal confirmation by the Cambridge town meeting, and the Governor signed this legislative act of March 17, 1846. On March 30, the town meeting ratified the act by a vote of 645 to 224. The town meeting which had made Cambridge law for more than two centuries met no more.

Not everyone was pleased with the way things turned out. The Old Cambridge loyalists entered the new alliance truculently. They were, however, relatively few in number and, on the whole, Cambridge adopted a spirit of conciliation. People were tired of the feud. Cambridgeport and East Cambridge, which had belonged to the speculators for years, were no longer hunks of real estate to be bought and sold and pierced by roads; they were vital communities with schools and churches and industries. Their residents did not have the same taste for battle that had motivated the old promoters, and they looked hopefully upon the city charter as a vehicle of cooperation. Symbolically, Cantabrigians chose a mayor with credentials which almost everyone could accept. James D. Green, an Old Cambridge resident, was a Harvard-educated clergyman, minister of the Unitarian church in East Cambridge. One of his first acts as head of the new city was to prohibit the pasturing of cows in Cambridge streets.

6

Fifty Years a City: Filling up the Spaces

Cambridge stood squarely in the path of immense forces—the industrial revolution, massive immigration, and railroad building—which combined to propel this once quaint and provincial town through fifty years of rapid growth and change. Though a standard nineteenth-century interpretation of growth was "progress," Cambridge suffered pains and vertigo along the way. The changes occurred so fast as to be beyond control, and civic authorities had all they could do to keep from being overwhelmed. When Cambridge celebrated its first half century as a city in 1896, it had become, more by default than by design, a modern, industrialized, sooty metropolis with a population density greater than Boston's.

A few statistics show the tremendous spurt that Cambridge industry took. The number of manufacturing firms increased at ten-year intervals as follows:

1845...94
1855...108
1865...173
1875...210
1885...578

Cambridge manufacturers employed 1,269 persons in 1845 and 14,258 in 1890. The more industries expanded or moved to Cambridge, the more immigrants came into the city—and vice versa, because industry and immigrants were mutually stimulating.

Cambridge population stood at 12,490 in 1845. By the end of the century that figure had doubled approximately three times up to nearly 100,000, not far below the population the city would have in the 1970s. Such awesome growth was not unique to Cambridge. Nearly every northeastern city with industrial potential experienced a mind-boggling multiplication.

Some of the new urban population in the Boston area came off the abandoned farms of New England. People gave up their tiresome battle with the soil, sold their land for a few dollars, and went in search of employment in the mill towns and expanding cities.

Even more people arrived from Europe, starting with the Irish. Since no one anticipated either the magnitude or the character of the foreign immigration, no preparations had been made, and the growth of cities was a matter of haphazard improvisation. The Harvard historian (and Cambridge resident) Oscar Handlin, in his book *Boston's Immigrants*, provides insight into the extraordinary effect that the Irish immigrants had upon Boston and neighboring communities. As Handlin explains, the Europeans who had migrated to New England during the eighteenth and early nineteenth centuries were, like the founding Puritans, reasonably well off. Passage to America cost money, and people who could afford the fare usually could pay to move inland beyond the populous coast to undeveloped lands or new settlements farther west. Those who wanted to farm headed for wide virgin lands. Many German, English, Norwegian, Swedish, and Scottish families disembarked in Boston, stocked up on provisions, and drove their wagons westward out of town. Immigrant artisans usually went elsewhere, too, because places like Boston and Cambridge were amply supplied with skilled labor, though a handful of English, German, and Scottish glassmakers did turn up in the glassworks in East Cambridge.

The Irish were the first of the tired, poor, "huddled masses" to reach American shores. They began arriving in substantial numbers around 1830. Expelled from their cottages and farms by landlords, then starved when the potato rot deprived them of their staple food in 1845, they fled Ireland by the hundreds of thousands. Transatlantic fares plummeted with the establishment of regular steamship service, and by the 1850s passage between Liverpool and Boston could be had for $20; but the Irish were so poor that $20 usually required a pooling of family resources. Landlords encouraged emigration and sometimes paid fares themselves because it cost them less to purchase boat tickets than to feed the poor.

The Irish who landed in Boston remained there because they had no means to proceed any farther. They were dispossessed peasants who had little exposure to the city and who, therefore, had no urban savvy. Many were illiterate and diseased. Most were bewildered. They crowded into unsanitary Boston cellars and makeshift tenement houses, and they worked at any job they could find.

The steamship companies, not the passengers, determined the port of entry. As for the Irish, they could hardly have arrived in a more disagreeable social climate. Boston was then supremely smug, perhaps justifiably so. Its prosperous, educated, hard-working, God-fearing citizens enjoyed a high standard of living. Boston was the acknowledged cultural center of the United States, a reputation for which it depended heavily upon Cambridge and Harvard. No city which thinks of itself as "the hub of the universe" or "the Athens of America" is modest. "The morality of Boston is more pure than that of any other city in America," wrote Bronson Alcott in 1828. In this context he clearly meant "Boston-and-Cambridge."

This self-esteem was produced by a people whose cultural assumptions and social order had not been severely challenged. Cambridge, for all its cosmopolitan intellectual activity, was a provincial society. The list of voters for the year 1822 included 481 names, of which only four sounded vaguely "foreign." Cantabrigians were almost uniformly Protestants of Anglo-Saxon descent. Unitarians and Congregationalists might split over religious issues, and indeed they did in the 1820s, forming two churches in Cambridge, both descended from the original parish church founded in 1636. (The Reverend Abiel Holmes departed from the old First Church in 1829 taking with him the orthodox portion of the congregation.) The Old Village, East Cambridge, and Cambridgeport might fight like wild dogs over a morsel of the town budget—and indeed they did. But these were family quarrels fought by family rules.

The Irish were emphatically not family. They were Roman Catholics and they were also poor, a combination of human conditions almost unknown in Cambridge. Neither their habits nor their traditions blended easily with American ways as practiced in the city. They trickled into East Cambridge over Craigie's Bridge—the first bridge in their path. A small Irish contingent had arrived in East Cambridge by the early 1830s. Irishmen worked in the fac-

The first Roman Catholic Church in Cambridge. This is St. John's, on Fourth Street in East Cambridge, built in 1842, demolished in 1934.

tories for subsistence wages, and Irishwomen worked as domestics. Since every family needed all the income it could get, parents often pulled their children out of school at the age of twelve or thirteen and sent them to work. At first the Irish went to church in Boston or Charlestown. Then, in 1831, a zealous convert, Daniel H. Southwick, began to agitate for a Catholic church in East Cambridge and started a Sunday School there. Ten years later, when there were 1,000 Irish living at the Point, money was finally raised for the building of Cambridge's first Roman Catholic church, St. John's.

Cambridge received the Irish cautiously. Factory owners took advantage of cheap, unskilled labor, and Cambridge householders rejoiced in the sudden availability of servants. Native New Englanders had been over-qualified and unwilling to work for low wages; so immigrant labor filled an economic void. But Cambridge regulars were uneasy with Roman Catholicism. Like many Americans, and like the Puritans of colonial days, they feared the Catholics' allegiance to the Pope. The activities of Southwick and other converts caused alarm; most Cantabrigians looked sourly upon the ardor of the Papists and of Protestants who transferred into Catholicism. Inevitably, some people felt more threatened than others. The morning after a band of Protestants burned the Ursuline Convent in Charlestown, Royal Morse, an auctioneer who lived in the Old Village, hurried from door to door to gather citizens to guard Harvard for fear that Catholics would set fire to the college buildings in retaliation. His precautions proved unnecessary, and calmer judgments took over. Judge Story led a meeting to protest the outrage in Charlestown and to affirm the rights of "our Catholic brethren." Similar meetings occurred in Boston and Charlestown as well, for many citizens were appalled by the barbaric act; but protests did not prevent further rioting in those cities, whereas Cambridge remained quiet. The American reverence for civil liberties muffled the fear of Catholicism. Cambridge never indulged in violent anti-Irish demonstrations.

In 1855 diehard conservatives in the Old Village revived their effort to withdraw from the rest of Cambridge, and the growing foreign population in East Cambridge was undoubtedly one of the reasons. In an odd twist, some East Cambridge residents also petitioned for separate status in the same year. This was the only section of the city with clear geographic integrity— nevertheless the reasons for this petition are not clear. The debate on division, argued before a committee of the state legislature, was so fierce that the *Cambridge Chronicle*, the local weekly which is still being published, declined to print it, "as the importance of cultivating and cherishing the most friendly relations between different sections of the city is far greater than the pleasure which we could give by the statement of evidence, or arguments of counsel, which, to say the least, would tend to widen the unfortunate difference which seems to exist among us, though by no means to the extent which some of the advocates of division appear to believe." The petitions failed.

The Yankees automatically assigned the Irish to the bottom of the social heap and treated the seventy-seven Negroes who lived in Cambridge (in 1840) with greater deference. The natives observed that the Irish drank and got into brawls. They had tuberculosis, and they were unskilled. In the refined atmosphere of Cambridge, they were a vulgar intrusion. The *Chronicle* used jokes about "Paddy" as space fillers; Paddy was usually pictured as a drunk or stupid. An East Cambridge-Irish reminiscence of the era noted of the Irish that "by reason of their race and creed they were practically a colony by themselves, their American neighbors having little in common with them, and although the social line was somewhat relaxed while attending school together, it was sharply drawn as they approached manhood." The city fulfilled its civic responsibilities by providing schools and relief for the poor, but the citizens of Anglo-Saxon descent felt no inclination to mingle with the Irish. As the Celtic population swelled in East Cambridge and inched up the slopes of Putnam Hill, the Yankee families who lived near the courthouse started to move to more elegant environs.

The Irish of the Boston area would have been in a social vacuum had it not been for the initiative of the Catholic Church. The Church provided a focal point and organizational medium for an uprooted people on strange soil. Added to its religious functions were many other roles. The Church helped people find jobs; it sponsored charitable relief; it published newspapers (the *Boston Pilot* and the *Boston Catholic Observer*) which influenced Irish opinions; it arranged social and cultural events. Catholic priests took the lead in representing the needs of their parishioners before civic authorities. As the Irish population increased and second-generation Irish acquired voting privileges, the Church emerged as a political force with which non-Catholics had to reckon.

Catholic organizations also attempted to remedy the acute problem of adult illiteracy among Irish immigrants. Children attended the public schools; not so their fathers and mothers. Educational efforts for the adult were entirely male-oriented. Illiterate mothers usually remained illiterate. In 1854, Father Lawrence Carroll, pastor of St. John's church in East Cambridge, started the "St. John's Literary Institute" in a loft above Fitzpatrick's butcher shop on Bridge Street. While Lowell, Longfellow, and Dr. Holmes discussed lofty ideas at the other end of town, full-grown Irishmen labored over spelling, punctuation, and multiplication tables at the institute's evening schools. Membership increased rapidly, and the society moved across the street to bigger and better quarters. The members contributed towards the formation of a library which was for many years the only circulating library in East Cambridge. The institute held debates, concerts, picnics, and lectures. The members put on plays, from farces to Shakespeare, formed a first-rate brass band, and sponsored community dances.

The growth of the Irish community in the 1850s coincided with America's worsening crisis over slavery. The question came up for debate in East Cambridge. In general, the Irish were not enthusiastic about the principle of emancipation. They were,

First Lieutenant John H. Rafferty, a member of St. John's Literary Institute in East Cambridge. He was an early casualty of the Civil War; he died at the battle of Malvern Hill on July 1, 1862.

however, committed to their new homeland. After the attack on Fort Sumter in 1861, they flocked to recruiting stations, a reaction which came naturally to a people who had seven centuries of conflict in their veins. The Civil War gave the Irish a chance to demonstrate their Americanism and shed the "foreign element" stigma. The St. John's Literary Institute threw itself into the war effort. When the call came for "nine-month" men during the summer of 1862, members organized the "Institute Guards" and volunteered their services to Cambridge Mayor Charles Russell, who disappointed them by stating that the city quota had already been filled. The unit disbanded and its members enlisted individually in scattered companies in Cambridge and Boston.

As their level of education improved, the Irish slowly gained some respect among Cambridge Yankees. In 1861 Harvard conferred an honorary degree upon Bishop J. B. Fitzpatrick of Boston, the first time a

FIFTY YEARS A CITY: FILLING UP THE SPACES

Catholic priest was thus honored. The wholehearted participation and bravery of the Irish in the defense of the Union eased the anxieties of those who worried lest a Catholic could not serve both Pope and country. By virtue of their numbers the Irish accumulated a latent political power. They slowly acquired the sophistication to use it. Socially, however, Irish circles seldom overlapped Yankee circles. The Church remained the pivotal point of the Irish community, and their society was introverted. Both Yankees and Irish seem to have been satisfied with this informal arrangement, for neither group was comfortable with the other.

Historically, the Irish got shortchanged by this bargain because the Yankees who wrote history were inclined to overlook them. Lucius Paige in his otherwise thorough *History of Cambridge* to the year 1877 never discussed the Irish presence except in peripheral references such as to the building of the Catholic churches. Yet by that date Irish-*born* individuals (that is, not including second-generation Irish) made up more than half the population of East Cambridge. In all, almost 8,000 Irish-born were Cantabrigians.

By then the Irish were not the only newcomers. The period after the Civil War brought Canadians—mostly Catholics of French, Irish, or Scottish origin. It also brought Portuguese who moved over from Boston's North End, Germans, Englishmen, Scots, and Swedes. The U.S. Census of 1880 counted the foreign-born population of Cambridge as: Irish, 8,366; British-American (that is, Canadians and West Indians), 3,981; English, 1,396; German, 636; Swedish, 169; Italian, 36; "Other Foreign-Born," 1,084. These figures added up to 15,668, compared with a total Cambridge population of 52,669. Among the "other foreign-born" were the Portuguese and a handful of Jews. Furthermore, a large number of black Americans arrived from the South, adding yet another dimension to the increasingly complex ethnic composition of the city. The *Chronicle*, having belabored the Irish for years, filled its humor column with jokes about others—blacks and Jews in particular. Blacks were depicted as childlike and slow-witted, Jews as smelly and shrewd. But the really important influx of non-Irish immigrants was to be a phenomenon of the twentieth century.

The spread of population throughout the new City of Cambridge proceeded with astonishing speed. When Lord Acton visited Cambridge in 1853, the physical appearance of the city did not impress him favorably. "I went in the omnibus to Cambridge," he noted in his diary. "We had to cross a long causeway, and the first thing we saw on the other side was the remains of several houses that had just burned down. We continued for about two miles between house and gardens, rather a solitary road, to Harvard College. Cambridge is a considerable town, but so scattered that there is nothing that can be called a street on it." No longer was Cambridge the compact and handsome place which had charmed another English visitor two centuries earlier. The Port, the Point, and the Old Village still stood apart from one another with open land between them, creating the diffused effect that had struck Lord Acton.

The open lands soon became childhood memories. Rail transportation greatly accelerated their development. The few years following Lord Acton's visit witnessed two events that foretold much about Cambridge's future. One was the opening in 1854 of a steam railroad, the Grand Junction, running down between East Cambridge and Cambridgeport, curving westward parallel to the Charles, and crossing the river at Cottage Farm where Boston University now stands and where a vehicular bridge had been constructed in 1850. The other event was the coming of an improved way to carry passengers along the streets from one section of the city to another—and to Boston. Horse-drawn cars rolling smoothly on rails began to supplant the horse-drawn omnibuses which had jolted along rough and muddy roads without benefit of tracks.

The Grand Junction was the first steam railroad to exert an important effect on Cambridge's factory districts, but it was not the first to enter the city. Others had

The Harvard Branch Railroad station, built in 1850. It became a student dining hall, Thayer Commons, when the railroad failed. It was torn down when Austin Hall, Harvard Law School, was built in 1883.

already passed through the edges of town. One of these lines connected Fresh Pond with the docks at Charlestown, cutting through North Cambridge on the way. It was built by the Charlestown Branch Railroad Company and its primary purpose was to haul ice from the pond, beginning in December 1841. By that time New England had a thriving business of shipping natural ice, packed in sawdust, for sale in southern markets such as New Orleans, Charleston, the West Indies, and even as far as India. Fresh Pond was an important center for the ice industry. It was there that the Tudor Ice Company, headed by Frederic Tudor, "the Ice King of New England," carried on one of its main operations. And it was there, in 1827, that Nathaniel Jarvis Wyeth, a young Cambridge man whose father owned the Fresh Pond Hotel, invented a horse-drawn ice cutter that transformed the industry.

The ice railroad was absorbed into the Fitchburg Railroad as it penetrated North Cambridge in 1843 on its way west. Since the Fitchburg brought no benefit to the industries in Cambridgeport or East Cambridge, local businessmen complained loudly of being bypassed by the railroads. The Harvard Branch Railroad, built in 1849 for passenger service, was equally useless to commercial interests. A locomotive and a single passenger car ran from the Fitchburg line in Somerville to a terminal which stood on a spot later occupied by Austin Hall at the Harvard Law School. The Harvard Branch facilitated travel between the Old Village and Boston but served too limited a clientele to survive. It was weakened by horse railway service and folded in 1855.

The Grand Junction had a sorry history of financial tangles, lawsuits, and bad luck. Service ended shortly after it had begun when a storm washed out the bridge

FIFTY YEARS A CITY: FILLING UP THE SPACES

at the foot of Brookline Street in Cambridgeport; it did not resume for eleven years, but the mere presence of a railroad attracted industries. By the late 1860s rail freight was moving profusely.

Meanwhile horse rail lines crisscrossed the city like a web woven by a drunken spider. Foster M. Palmer reconstructed the networks in his paper called "Horse Car, Trolley, and Subway" (Cambridge Historical Society *Proceedings*, 1961-1963). Street railways had existed in New York, New Orleans, and Carrollton, Louisiana, since the 1830s, but Boston and Cambridge were the New England pioneers of this type of transportation. The first horse rail line in Cambridge arrived from Boston across the West Boston Bridge, ran the length of Main Street (including that portion now called Massachusetts Avenue), through Harvard Square, out Brattle Street to Mount Auburn

Horse cars change the look of Cambridge.
This is Lafayette Square (where Main Street now meets Massachusetts Avenue) about 1858. The First Universalist Church, at left, is shown as remodeled in that year. In 1888 it was moved six blocks westward to 8 Inman Street. Later its steeple was removed; still later it became a Syrian Orthodox Church.

Cemetery. Service began along this line in April 1856. It was a huge success, and new lines followed shortly after: on River Street, Cambridge Street, Garden Street–Concord Avenue–Craigie Street, and north on Massachusetts Avenue into North Cambridge and Arlington. By 1875 horse cars left Harvard Square every seven minutes for Boston's Bowdoin Square via Main Street; there was half-hourly service to Bowdoin Square via Broadway, and to Scollay Square via Cambridge Street and the Canal Bridge.

After some thirty years of horse cars the electric trolley arrived on the Cambridge scene, pulling the neighborhoods even closer together. During the 1890s the electrification of the street railways of American cities proceeded with astonishing speed. Boston and Cambridge were in the forefront, beginning their first trolley lines early in 1889, one year behind Richmond, Virginia, which was the pioneer. In only a few years the electric cars, much speedier and noisier than those pulled by horses, had supplanted all the horse-drawn cars on Cambridge streets. Almost the last to go were the horse cars on Brattle Street, where the residents strongly opposed the idea of poles, trolley wires, and the roar of the heavier cars. The problem was solved by putting trolleys on Mount Auburn Street instead, and Brattle Street had no street railways of any kind after the summer of 1894. Electric streetcars were a conspicuous part of Cambridge life for nearly seventy years, criss-crossing the city and carrying passengers to the neighboring towns. Finally in 1958 the last of them succumbed to trackless trolleys and buses.

Thus, beginning in the 1850s, trains and streetcars revitalized Cambridge commercial life, restored the good humor of its businessmen, and dictated the character and direction of the city's development. They confirmed Cambridge's status as a thoroughfare to Boston; and the existence of inexpensive public transport put Cambridge within commuting distance for the poorer immigrants who looked for jobs there. Moreover, the street railways opened new areas of the city to settlement. Streets were laid out near the lines. Houses and tenements to accommodate the growing population sprang up north of Cambridge Street, north of Harvard Square (by mid-century known by that name), and out in the direction of Fresh Pond. Cambridge began to sprawl over its territory in random fashion. The combination of immigrants and rails changed Cambridge into a modern industrial city. Either factor alone could not have accomplished the job, for industry needed both cheap labor and efficient means of distribution.

Many of the new Cantabrigians lived in boarding houses or rented cheap flats in the multiple-family wooden houses that were appearing all over town (and were still standing in large numbers as late as the 1970s). Some of the newcomers bought land and built small homes. They settled near their places of employment and along the transportation lines. Only the Old Village remained off limits to the poor by virtue of its high real estate values, but occasionally a prosperous foreigner moved within its precincts. Though people of the same national origin sometimes formed small clusters, no genuine ethnic "ghettos" appeared—partly because the street railways distributed people throughout the city, partly because there was a great deal of moving from one place to another. Families who improved their financial status moved to a better part of town or even to another town. This was the pattern not only for the immigrants but also for Americans who had left rural areas for the city. Homeowners were more likely to stay in one spot than tenants, but there was still a regular and sizable turnover of residents in Cambridgeport and East Cambridge. The principal turnover in Old Cambridge was in the population of college students.

In 1875 the *Chronicle* said of East Cambridge: "Probably there is no place of its size where so great a change has taken place in the class of inhabitants, a large proportion of the families who resided here fifteen years ago having moved away, and strangers, among whom are included a large foreign element, taken their places."

The rail and waterfront facilities of

FIFTY YEARS A CITY: FILLING UP THE SPACES

Bird's-eye drawing of East Cambridge in 1879 discloses vigorous industrial activity. You are looking approximately southwest. In lower left corner is where the Canal (Craigie) Bridge begins. The right side of the picture shows parts of Somerville. The long train at upper middle of picture is headed toward Cambridgeport, which is visible all across background, beyond the open spaces. The train's last car has just crossed Cambridge Street, which begins at lower left and disappears on the far horizon at extreme upper right, where, with a magnifying glass, you may be able to make out two or three spires of Old Cambridge. A slice of the Back Bay section of Boston can be faintly seen at extreme upper left, across the Charles.

East Cambridge had made it a prime industrial location and caused an upheaval in population. In the 1850s many Yankee professional men and business leaders lived there, including two of the six richest men in Cambridge, Jesse Hall, who owned a lumberyard, and Samuel Parker, a Boston businessman. But people of that sort moved out as big and sometimes obnoxious factories moved in. The once balanced population tipped in the direction of unskilled labor. John P. Squire started a modest meat-packing plant on a few acres along Miller's Creek in 1855. (The creek has since been filled.) When Squire's slaughtered only one hog a day it did not influence the character of the neighborhood; but when the operation had expanded to 22 acres and 2,500 hogs per day—and a labor force of one thousand—it became one of the most noticeable features in the East Cambridge landscape. Boston's James Curley once called Cambridge "a pig sticking village."

The glass manufacturers, originally the biggest industry there, slowly declined because of competition from states farther west. New England Glass collapsed in 1888. Edward Libbey, the firm's head, shut down the works after a disastrous series of labor disputes and moved to Toledo, Ohio, with about one hundred workmen. The glassworks chimney, taller than the Bunker Hill monument, stood until 1921 when it crumbled beneath the chisels and mallets of a wrecking crew.

The glassworks' demise, however, scarcely diminished the industrial vitality of the Point. The list of industries located there in 1890 included—besides Squire's meat-packing company—the Boston Bridge Works, American Net & Twine (fishnets), William L. Lockhart & Co. (caskets), Goepper Brothers (barrels), Revere Sugar, John C. Dow & Co. (fertilizer), and

John P. Squire & Company, the pork-packing plant in East Cambridge, in its heyday around the turn of the century. This plant was on Gore Street, on property straddling the Somerville line. The electric streetcars at right are on Bridge Street, which became Somerville Avenue a little farther along.

FIFTY YEARS A CITY: FILLING UP THE SPACES

several furniture manufacturers.

Although East Cambridge industry contributed substantially to the economic health of the entire city, it did not enhance the residential qualities of the immediate neighborhood. Noisy, dirty, smelly factories formed a ring around the grid of streets which, though lined with mostly cheaply built houses and tenements, were not altogether unpleasant. The Point offered no opportunities for the man who improved himself or for his children who were educated and skilled. East Cambridge was a place to get a start and to leave, if not in the first generation, then in the second. But even people who had been eager to escape its industrial confines often looked back at East Cambridge affectionately, remembering baseball games and church outings and loafing on street corners and good neighbors—forgetting how dreadful it had been to be poor. Some of them called themselves "Dearos," for "Dear Old East Cambridge Residents." Meanwhile, new people moved in to replace those who had moved up and out.

Cambridgeport, a big area of several parts, remained predominantly residential until the mid-1850s when the promise of the railroad attracted industry. Soon Cambridgeport was manufacturing candy, boxes, metal goods, wire, biscuits, and hosiery—along with the inevitable soap with which its industrial history had started. The factories and the unskilled workers which they employed tended to endow pockets of Cambridgeport with an East Cambridge atmosphere. But the Port also employed semi-skilled and skilled workers, for example in its printing house (the Riverside Press), book bindery (Little, Brown & Co.), and piano and organ factory (Mason & Hamlin), and in the production of telescopes at Alvan Clark & Sons.

The Riverside Press was especially interesting because it was part of Cambridge's return to prominence as a printing center. The original Cambridge press had ceased operating in 1692, and for more than a century hardly any printing was done in Cambridge. But by 1896 the city had three of America's leading book printers. The Riverside Press was one of these, a cluster of buildings on the river bank between Western Avenue and River Street where the Charles flows southward. It was owned by the Boston publishing house Houghton, Mifflin & Company (later called Houghton Mifflin Company) and indeed had been the publishing firm's parent—its first proprietor having been Henry O. Houghton in 1852. Another of the trio of book printers was the University Press, in Old Cambridge. Harvard had founded it in 1802 and sold it in 1827. In private hands it expanded greatly and moved into a former hotel in Brattle Square in 1865, then built larger quarters a little closer to the river in 1895. The third important printer in 1896 was the Athenaeum Press, owned by the Boston publisher Ginn & Company and located in a brand-new building on the Cambridgeport–East Cambridge borderline, facing the Charles. All three of these thriving shops have vanished in the twentieth century.

Industry brought people to Cambridgeport. The population there increased by approximately 10,000 each decade between 1865 and 1895, always accounting for almost precisely half of the entire Cambridge population. St. Mary's, the first Roman Catholic church in Cambridgeport, was dedicated in 1868 at Harvard and Norfolk Streets; and a second was necessary within five years. As employment opportunities opened in Cambridge, fewer people crossed the river to jobs in Boston, and the Port approached economic self-sufficiency.

Like East Cambridge, Cambridgeport had to produce housing under pressure. Building speculators put up tenements and houses almost as fast as the New York Biscuit Company on Main Street turned out cookies. By the 1870s streets and houses occupied Judge Dana's former property south of the present Massachusetts Avenue, and Cambridgeport edged closer to the Old Village until the "huckleberry pastur" of yesteryear disappeared.

Though Cambridgeport was in some respects similar to East Cambridge, it never belonged so completely to industry and industrial workers. Nineteenth-century

The First Baptist Church in Central Square, built in 1866. It burned down in 1881 and was immediately replaced by a new church which remains there today. Notice the horse car.

Tenement buildings such as this housed many of the people who flooded Cambridge in the late nineteenth and early twentieth centuries. This block, on Main Street, was built in 1873 and torn down in 1957.

FIFTY YEARS A CITY: FILLING UP THE SPACES

Cambridgeport sprawled over the territory which included the agreeable residential section west of Prospect Street and north of Massachusetts Avenue (an area which the Cambridge Historical Commission assigns to "Mid Cambridge" for practical purposes). Central Square, Inman Square, Kendall Square, Main Street, and Massachusetts Avenue were commercially thriving. Many store owners, clerks, secretaries, bank tellers, and municipal employees lived in the Port. The *Cambridge Chronicle* had its offices there; it was the city's most influential newspaper, most of the time its *only* newspaper. There were doctors and dentists and lawyers. Mrs. E. A. Dickenson, who described herself as a "clairvoyant, physician, business and test medium" held seances on Cottage Street. The Cambridge Conservatory of Music was on Lee Street.

Cambridgeport was partly attractive, partly ugly, always hard to characterize in a few words. The biggest, most thriving section of Cambridge, it had a wide range of residents—Yankees and Negroes and foreigners—with an equally wide range of talents and income. East Cambridge residents gravitated towards Boston, but Port

The bicycle craze comes to Cambridge. This photograph was taken at the Cambridgeport Cycle Club in Central Square, on Main Street (now Massachusetts Avenue) at Pearl Street, around 1889.

people had ties with the Old Village as well. Protestant churches flourished beside the Catholic. Cambridgeport was perhaps best described by the social scientist Albert Kennedy, who called it "a condition of life midway between East Cambridge and Old Cambridge."

North Cambridge is that section presently bounded on the northeast by the Somerville line running parallel to Massachusetts Avenue beyond Porter Square; on the north by Arlington at the Alewife Brook Parkway; on the west by Belmont beyond Fresh Pond; and on the south by Huron Avenue and Upland Road. In the nineteenth century North Cambridge was the least densely populated, most overlooked part of the city. During Cambridge's first two centuries, North Cambridge was sparsely settled and

The cattle market in North Cambridge, drawn by Winslow Homer for *Ballou's Pictorial Drawing Room Companion,* July 2, 1859. The illustration appeared with the following explanation: "Porter's farfamed hotel is seen in the centre of the middle distance with its extensive stables, the cattle pens being in the rear of it. There are extensive pasturage grounds in the vicinity. The fair for the sale of these dumb victims . . . takes place every Wednesday . . . The cattle in the pens seem to have a prophetic vision of the fate reserved for them, and the bellowing of cows and oxen, blended with the bleating of sheep and the grunting of pigs, makes up a concert which would drive an Italian musician mad. Interesting specimens of humanity are also to be seen at these fairs, and altogether they are well worth visiting by mere lookers-on."

traversed only by a few roads towards the outlying villages. Its most prominent landmark was Porter's Tavern, which gave its name to Porter Square, Porterhouse steak, and, as known to venturesome Harvard undergraduates, a concoction known as Porter's flip which packed a wicked wallop. The cattle market settled in North Cambridge in the 1830s—after the enclosing of the Common where farmers had formerly rested their animals—and gave rise to taverns, inns, stockyards, a slaughterhouse, and a race track called the "Trotting Park" which covered a large tract just north of the present Rindge Avenue.

The Fitchburg Railroad of 1843 intruded on the country-fair scene. While rail-less Cambridge businessmen were grumbling in other parts of town, eagle-eyed real estate speculators interpreted the activity of the cattle market and the railroad as signals to begin their work. Gilman Sargent quickly acquired the Philemon Russell estate, chopped it into building lots, laid out Russell and Orchard streets near Somerville, and made money on the transaction. The purchase and division of other tracts continued at a rapid pace, and streets were carved out with little attention to large-scale organization.

FIFTY YEARS A CITY: FILLING UP THE SPACES

Because industry preferred the conveniences of waterfront sites close to the bridges to Boston, only one manufacturing industry located in North Cambridge: brick making, which took advantage of the clay subsoil. The Bay State Brick Company arrived in 1863, followed by five more brick companies before the end of the century. Otherwise North Cambridge was largely residential. The cattle market and related facilities closed in 1868.

When the horse cars put North Cambridge within commuting range of Cambridgeport, East Cambridge, and Boston, it began to attract people who worked in the factories. Port and Point residents who had built up savings accounts moved out of the tenements and relocated in the quieter, more attractive surroundings of North Cambridge. Though there were people from all ethnic backgrounds, the neighborhood had a strong concentration of "lace-curtain" Irish—as the Irish called their more prosperous brothers—and of French Canadians who collected there to work in the brick yards.

North Cambridge did not develop in any consequential fashion. It grew in response to Cambridge's expanding population and without the more precise intentions that had generated Cambridgeport and East Cambridge. It had no definite focal point, such as Harvard Square or Central Square, and it had no courthouse or city hall. After the closing of the cattle market, Porter Square emerged as a minor commercial center, but many North Cambridge residents crossed the Somerville town line and did their business at Davis Square. Yet the population was quite stable. Neighbors knew one another, their children married and stayed in North Cambridge, and this newest section of the city developed a stronger community solidarity than existed in any other part of Cambridge save in the Old Village.

Of all Cambridge's disjointed parts, Old Cambridge was the least directly affected by the industrial boom. In 1873, only four manufacturers were located there: the Jones Carriage Company on the corner of Church and Palmer streets, a planing mill on Boylston Street, the Reversible Collar Company on Arrow Street, and the University Press in Brattle Square. The most vigorous "industry" in Old Cambridge was Harvard University, and Harvard set the tone of the community.

In 1869, when Charles William Eliot became president, Harvard had just over a thousand students, graduate and undergraduate. By 1896 the number had jumped to nearly 3,000. The university included Harvard College, the graduate school, the Lawrence Scientific School, and schools of law, medicine, divinity, veterinary medicine, agriculture, and horticulture. Separate and not quite equal was Radcliffe College, which opened in 1879 under the name of the Society for the Collegiate Instruction of Women, with Harvard professors doing the teaching.

University expansion and building kept apace with enrollment. Having purchased lands, especially to the north and east of its "Yard," Harvard owned 82 acres by 1896. Among the new academic buildings and dormitories, too numerous to list here, Memorial Hall was easily the most visible. This ornate cathedral-like concoction, topped by a 190-foot tower, was built in the early 1870s and dedicated to Harvard men who had died in the Civil War. At the west end of Memorial Hall sat John Harvard in bronze, the work of Daniel Chester French. Because no one knew what John Harvard had looked like, the face was modeled from that of young Sherman Hoar. In 1899 the statue was moved into Harvard Yard at the west side of University Hall.

Old Cambridge was the most attractive residential quarter of the city, an area of charm, tradition, and grace enhanced by the dignified presence of the college. It drew business and professional men from other parts of Cambridge and from Boston, people who had acquired tastes for gracious living and a stimulating intellectual climate and the financial capability to gratify them. The new population was often, but not necessarily, American; increasingly there were distinguished foreigners and a smattering of Irish. Amid professorial homes

The evolution of Memorial Hall. This massive structure is more than a Harvard building — for more than a century it has been a Cambridge landmark, conspicuous at the convergence of Broadway, Cambridge Street, and Kirkland Street. UPPER LEFT: The 190-foot tower in 1874 when the building was brand-new. UPPER RIGHT: Ornamentation and a four-faced clock were added in 1897, as shown in a twentieth-century picture. The tower was being renovated on September 6, 1956, when it was destroyed by fire, the clock plunging into the lobby. The large photo was taken in 1972. The parts of the building not shown are Alumni Hall to the left and Sanders Theatre to the right. For a view of the whole structure see the aerial picture on page 7.

FIFTY YEARS A CITY: FILLING UP THE SPACES

they built pleasant houses northward toward the Harvard botanical garden and the new Harvard College Observatory, between Brattle Street and Huron Avenue, and off Kirkland and Oxford streets near the new Harvard buildings. The Shady Hill and Dana Hill sections developed as a spiritual extension of Old Cambridge under the influence of university expansion and certain building restrictions written into deeds; by now, no one considers these areas as "Cambridgeport."

Poor people were scarce in the Old Village. Young instructors at the college struggled along on low salaries in genteel poverty that had nothing in common with the poverty of black or immigrant families in East Cambridge or Cambridgeport. Though the straightest trip from Old Cambridge to Boston traversed East Cambridge or Cambridgeport, residents and students from Old Cambridge who made the trip may not have noticed the rest of the city. Such separation as had been denied by the General Court had been achieved by the imperatives of economics.

Harvard Square was the heart of Old Cambridge. Omnibus and then horse-car lines converged there. Shops catering to students and the community—barbers, tobacconists, bookstores, taverns, and so on—congregated and spilled over into Boylston Street and Brattle Square. A Harvard Square bookseller named John Bartlett produced the first edition of his *Familiar Quotations* in 1855, and the book grew fatter and more famous as edition followed edition.

Old Cambridge had a special aura. William Dean Howells, who moved to Cambridge when he joined the *Atlantic Monthly* in 1866, wrote that "even the question of family, which is of so great concern in New England, was in abeyance. Perhaps it was taken for granted that everyone in Old Cambridge society must be of good family, or he could not be there; perhaps his mere residence tacitly ennobled him; certainly his acceptance was an informal patent of gentility. To my mind, the structure of society was almost ideal."

This almost ideal society had been shaken, in 1849, by the greatest scandal in Harvard history. Dr. George Parkman was seen entering the Harvard Medical School, then in Boston's West End, on the afternoon of Friday, November 23; no one ever admitted to seeing him alive again. One week later a janitor cut a hole in a brick wall in the basement of the Medical School and revealed parts of a human corpse. Police arrested Harvard Professor John White Webster in his Cambridge home later that night. Dr. Webster was tried for the murder, found guilty, and hanged on August 30, 1850. Cambridge and Harvard were in an uproar. To this day there are people who believe Webster's fervent plea of innocence.

People like William Dean Howells made Cambridge a literary mecca, but the most dramatic intellectual event of the latter nineteenth century occurred in scientific circles: it was the debate over Darwinism. A Swiss immigrant, Louis Agassiz, already renowned for his brilliant theory of the Ice Age, accepted the chair of natural history at Harvard's Lawrence Scientific School in 1848 and went on to found Harvard's famous Museum of Comparative Zoology in 1859. Agassiz, a persuasive man and a born showman, became one of the most glamorous figures in Cambridge. While he was promoting the study of geology and zoology, the botanist Asa Gray worked thoughtfully in his house at the botanical garden just off Garden Street. Gray's research and his familiarity with the unpublished theories of Charles Darwin led him into direct conflict with Agassiz. The Swiss stuck by his background of German idealism and his statement that "a species is a thought of the Creator." Gray understood the scientific merit of evolution through natural selection. In the spring of 1860, after Darwin's work had been published, the two men clashed in public debate. The great Agassiz, while retaining the faith of his public, lost face among his colleagues and grew old in bitterness. Gray went on to be the most prominent botanist in the United States.

Henry Wadsworth Longfellow was known to every American school child, and literary men of the western world sought him out in the lovely house on Brattle Street where George Washington had planned

FIFTY YEARS A CITY: FILLING UP THE SPACES

strategy to evict the British from Boston. Old Cambridge collected stars in a dazzling intellectual constellation. "Why," exclaimed Bret Harte, who lived there briefly, "you couldn't fire a revolver from your front porch anywhere without bringing down a two-volumner!"

Harvard Square in the 1850s. Commercial activity was increasing fast. You are looking approximately west, from the college yard down Brattle Street. The Cambridge Gas Light Company occupied the Lyceum Building at the right. The Harvard Coop, a consumer-cooperative department store, stands there now.

Across the Charles, Boston had experienced Cambridge's growing pains on a larger scale, and by the turn of the century there were half a million Bostonians. During the 1850s, pushed by the great Irish influx, Boston had started extending its physical area by filling the tidal marshes north of the Boston Neck and creating an elegant residential district which is still known as the Back Bay.

Cambridge coexisted with the ragged, sludgy edges of the Charles somewhat longer. Squatter settlements—called "tin villages"—grew up on some of the marshlands. Cambridge's most desperate citizens improvised rudimentary housing on spots that were not directly exposed to tidal influences and used their few household wastes for fill. Municipal authorities turned their backs on these unwholesome settlements until sanitary conditions presented a threat to the city at large. Meanwhile, various development groups, envious of the success of Boston's Back Bay, evolved reclamation schemes which were interrupted by a financial panic during the 1870s. When the economy picked up during the eighties, the plans were revived, and now the dwindling of good building lots in Cambridge added a new impetus.

The most ambitious of the development groups was the Charles River Embankment Company, which proposed a plan to convert 215 acres bounded by the river, Main Street, and the Grand Junction Railroad tracks into a residential area similar to the Back Bay. The design included the building of a sea wall from the West Boston Bridge to the Brookline (Cottage Farm) Bridge, landfill behind the wall, a residential section set along a broad esplanade, and—critical—a new bridge to Boston. The first thousand feet of sea wall was built in 1883. After much haggling, the new bridge was completed in 1889 and opened to traffic a year later. It was called the Harvard Bridge, a name which now is confusing because, though it carries Massachusetts Avenue, which eventually leads to Harvard, the first stop on the Cambridge side is M.I.T. A new financial depression hit in 1893 and hurt the developers seriously; reclamation work slowed down to a crawl.

Henry M. Whitney, real estate speculator of Brookline, Massachusetts, bought riverfront properties in East Cambridge in 1889, built a sea wall eastward, and took on the task of reclaiming marshes and mudflats in that section of Cambridge.

As for the Charles, it had become worse than unsightly; it was noxious. The sewage pollution got worse and worse by the year, and people living near the river began to agitate. During the summer of 1892 hundreds of Old Cambridge folk and all the practicing physicians in the vicinity of Harvard Square petitioned the Board of Health "praying that some relief might be given from a condition of things believed to be positively injurious to health, and known to be so offensive that windows had to be closed during the period of low tide on the river." They waited twenty years before their prayers were answered by the damming of the Charles.

Reacting to improvements in Boston, where Frederick Law Olmsted had created a handsome system of public parks and had spoken eloquently of the necessity for green spaces in cities, Cambridge formed a municipal park commission in 1892. The commission employed Charles Eliot, landscape architect, to make a plan for a Cambridge park system. His report recommended a park along the whole of the Charles River from the Canal Bridge to the Watertown line with a river road (Memorial Drive) extended to Fresh Pond and connected along Alewife Brook to the Mystic River. The plan also called for playgrounds spaced across the city. Surveying the existing and proposed changes in Cambridge's topography in 1896, one writer predicted that "there can now be no retrograde action in the treatment of the beautiful river." After years of turning its back upon the Charles, Cambridge was shifting its position. The twentieth century would bring the finishing touches.

7

Fifty Years a City: Coming of Age

On Monday—or it could have been a Tuesday—workmen laid a dozen more yards of track on Cambridge Street; carpenters finished the roof on a house in Cambridgeport; bricklayers heightened the north wall of the Museum of Comparative Zoology on Oxford Street; digging progressed for the foundations of a factory on the riverbank; a woman died in childbirth in East Cambridge but an Irish family straggled across a bridge from Boston; a 19-year-old black man arrived from South Carolina; a couple came into town from a Vermont farm. Day by day, in small increments but relentlessly, the growth went on. And somebody had to cope with it.

Even in their most fanciful dreams, Judge Francis Dana, Andrew Craigie, Royal Makepeace, and Rufus Davenport had never calculated on this scale. James Russell Lowell, returning to Cambridge from a trip to Europe during the 1860s, wrote to a friend: "You wouldn't know Cambridge with its railroad and its waterworks and its new houses . . . I seem to see our dear old village wriggling itself out of its chrysalis and balancing its green wings till the sun gives them color and firmness." He had lost his romantic boyhood Cambridge, but he loved the new one too and gave it the gift of his lovely metaphor. Others, however, were less enchanted. "I confess I do not like this process of suburbanization,—or the results of it," wrote Charles Eliot Norton to his cousin Charles William Eliot in 1864. "The old town was better in the days when we were boys, my dear Charles!"

As factory chimneys competed with church steeples in the skyline, growth made people and institutions rich. Real estate speculators, builders, merchants, industrialists, bankers, railroad barons, church parishes, and Harvard University benefited handsomely. Growth made the less rich more comfortable, for it created jobs for factory workers, bartenders, secretaries, cooks, scullery maids, civil servants, engineers, doctors, and lawyers. The Irish kept sending back to the old country for their relatives because they knew it was better to be poor in Cambridge where there was hope than to starve in Ireland where there was none. As long as the economic curve kept rising, nobody complained about growth. Questions were raised only if the curve went off course. When business hesitated during the "Great Depression" of 1873-1878, the *Chronicle* urged immigration westward with the admonition that "the hordes of European day-laborers who are being thrown upon our shores by the steamship lines make a great mistake when they settle down on the Eastern coast and attempt to make a living where the avenues are already choked by their predecessors." But the "Great Depression" hardly made a dent in Cambridge, and the curve shot up again. Cambridge mayors flourished growth figures as evidence that the city was marching onwards through civilization.

The municipal government was exactly where it was supposed to be: one step behind the growth. Cambridge development remained in the hands of businessmen who did not want to be told where they should draw streets or build factories. Free enterprise enjoyed liberty and immense power. The city had no planning department, no building code, and no zoning laws. The Puritan founders, with their regulations on setbacks and roofing materials and their requirements to fill in all vacant lots before enlarging the town, had endowed the development process with some order. Nineteenth-century Cambridge did not control. It coped. But on the whole it coped well.

George Rufus Cook commented on the philosophy of government in Cam-

Museum of Comparative Zoology as photographed about 1875 from the tower of Memorial Hall. Camera points north, and Oxford Street slants across left side of picture. Eventually this building grew into the University Museum (actually five separately administered Harvard museums). It was built in eleven sections between 1859 and 1913; this photograph shows the first two stages.

FIFTY YEARS A CITY: COMING OF AGE

bridge in the days before the city charter: "Cambridge held itself responsible for the education of its youth and for the care of its destitute. There was also a languid attempt to furnish protection to the property and lives of its inhabitants through police and fire departments, and here, in great measure, the functions of a municipal government, as then conceived, ended. All other means of administering to the necessities, the comfort, or the happiness of the people, were left to individual or corporate effort, and what those agencies failed to supply was left unsupplied." Such philanthropic organizations as the Cambridge Humane Society, founded by the good Dr. Abiel Holmes in 1814, cared for poor and ailing citizens. The Society had once loaned out "bathing tubs" by the week to borrowers who were warned to return them clean and dry and who had to pay a ten-cent fine for every day beyond the specified time. Churches undertook to provide for their needy parishioners.

This quaint system had worked well enough when Cambridge was small, but, as the population expanded, public necessities surpassed the capabilities of private individuals and the charitable instincts of corporations. The Cambridge of 1846 had vast needs. It lacked paving, curbs, and lighting on its streets. There was no sewer system, street cleaning, or waste collection. Drinking water came from private wells. There was no public library. Though a fire department had existed since 1832, it operated on a parsimonious budget and was composed chiefly of volunteers. When City Hall caught fire in 1853, it was completely destroyed because the engines were unable to reach the building through deep snow. (Snow removal in Cambridge did not begin until the twentieth century. Despite the city's efforts, snow-clogged streets remain a chronic winter problem, supplying local newsmen with wisecracks in the absence of more exciting news.) City Hall was no tragic loss. The municipal government had already outgrown it and, luckily, the records survived the fire. The authorities moved to the new Cambridge Athenaeum, at Massachusetts Avenue and Pleasant Street, and stayed there until 1890 when they occupied

Early snow removal in Cambridge was of the do-it-yourself kind. This is Trowbridge Street on a bleak day in 1894.

the present City Hall on the other side of the avenue.

The list of services which Cambridge did not provide in 1846 continues: there was no city physician and no public health or sanitation facilities. The first city budget allowed $46.66 for "health." Such machinery as existed for caring for the indigent, infirm, or aged was totally inadequate.

Cantabrigians transferred these burdens to the city government reluctantly. The habit of self-sufficiency and of the town meeting, where everyone had his say and his vote, died hard. But as the problems of urban living assumed proportions which defied private solutions, Cambridge citizens expanded their interpretation of the role of government.

The story of the police department illustrated the Cambridge attitude perfectly. In 1845 the town had three constables, one each in East Cambridge, Cambridgeport, and Old Cambridge. When the new-fangled notion of a police force was put before the new City Councillors and Aldermen in 1846, Mayor James Green is supposed to have muttered, "let every man keep a dog instead." Some Cantabrigians agreed with him. Crime had never been a

London bobbies? No, Cambridge police as they looked in the tall-helmet era, standing at police headquarters, Central Square, in 1915.

serious problem in the town, and they feared that the police would interfere with their liberties. But the Council passed the ordinance, citing the rise of property valuations and population. Cambridge got its first police force: seven constables, seven watchmen, and a night policeman named Day. For a few years the force kept busy arresting reckless drivers, particularly on Sundays and racing days when out-of-towners came to Cambridge to frolic. Then crimes against property began to increase, and by 1871 the city had a force of fifty, usually criticized for doing too little rather than too much.

During the first fifty years of its incorporation, 1846 to 1896, the City of Cambridge: built an almshouse and infirmary; undertook the seemingly endless process of repairing and paving the streets (modern man's equivalent of perpetual motion); collected ashes and household refuse; constructed a city-wide sewer system; provided benefits for sick or disabled Civil War veterans; established a city water supply; appointed a Clerk of Committees, a City Auditor, and a Superintendent of Public Buildings and Inspector of Buildings. In 1888 Cambridge was enjoying over a thousand gas, kerosene, and electric lights on its streets, yielding dim illumination and a pretty twinkle. It was in 1892, with open space becoming scarce, that the City Council created the Board of Park Commissioners, which set in motion the ambitious plan for a network of parks and playgrounds throughout Cambridge. All this cost money, and the city budget increased from less than $41,000 in 1846 to $2,500,000 in 1896. Predictably there was some grumbling about the tax rate, which rose from $5 per thousand to $17.50 during the same period—figures to make the present Cambridge taxpayer weep with envy—but taxes always cause grumbling.

Throughout Cambridge's history, the largest single expenditure was that for the support of the schools. For a town as fanatic as Cambridge about education, the public school system had become surprisingly tattered. What had been an excellent program by the standards of the times started to deteriorate early in the nineteenth century when the development of East Cambridge and Cambridgeport made it necessary to build new schools in those areas. Separate schools in separate parts of town reinforced the rivalry among the three sections and made every appropriation for education a political hot potato. Furthermore, the town fell badly behind during the sudden upsurge in population between 1840 and 1845. Many school buildings were old, drafty, and leaky. Teachers presided over unwieldy numbers of children; the average size of a grammar school class was seventy-one. Yet approximately 25 percent of Cambridge children did not go to school at all. Compared with neighboring cities, Cambridge did not give generously toward education. In 1845 Cambridge spent $3.95 per child as opposed to $5.09 in Charlestown, $6.76 in Boston, and $7.64 in Somerville.

Co-education, already practiced in some other Massachusetts towns, was not adopted in Cambridge public schools until 1845. The innovation prompted hysterical reactions among some Cantabrigians. When schools opened under the new rules in 1846, distraught parents besieged the School Committee with threats to remove their daughters from the classrooms and with bizarre schemes for safeguarding their purity. One ingenious father proposed that "squinting boards" be erected between boys and girls to prevent them from exchanging "sheeps' eyes" during lessons. But the fuss died down as people adjusted to the idea, and co-education proceeded on schedule.

The new city government tried to resolve old enmities by reshuffling the schools. In 1847 the first central high school opened in Cambridgeport to replace the former system of three high schools. The School Committee hoped that the mixing of children from different parts of the city would diffuse sectional jealousies. City Councillors from Old Cambridge opposed the plan, and of the seventy-four students who appeared at the school on opening day, only one—the Mayor's daughter—lived in Old Cambridge. The boycott lasted a year during which Old Village parents sent their children to the neighborhood school; but when the city closed that school in 1848, Old Cambridge children joined their peers in the central high school.

Though faced with the population explosion, an insufficiency of good teachers, and buildings which became overcrowded years ahead of plan, Cambridge succeeded in upgrading and broadening the standard of public education. By 1896 the number of pupils per teacher in grammar schools dropped to thirty-eight, even while the total number of students climbed from two to ten thousand. Textbooks, curriculum, buildings, and classroom techniques were all substantially improved. Massachusetts law admitted black children into the school system in 1855. During the early 1880s, a black woman named Maria Baldwin, who had attended the training school for teachers in Cambridge, stunned the School Committee by applying for a teaching position. The air in the room thickened with embarrassment until one committeeman finally stood up and said, "Look, we've allowed Miss Baldwin to take this course. She's done it with credit, and she deserves a position." Baldwin was assigned to the Agassiz School on Oxford Street. She later became its Master and organized the first parent-teacher group in Cambridge.

Improved or not, public schooling did not satisfy everyone, and a proliferation of private schools occurred simultaneously with public school expansion. There was the old Cambridgeport Private Grammar School of 1828, attended by Richard Henry Dana, Margaret Fuller, and Oliver Wendell Holmes (the doctor, not his son the jurist). Louis Agassiz and his wife ran an exceptional school in their home between 1855 and 1863. Called the Agassiz School, it was the institution for which Maria Baldwin's public school was named. Joshua Kendall's Day and Family School groomed young gentlemen for Harvard. In 1883 Harvard men founded the progressive Browne and Nichols school, a "Fitting and Developing School for Boys," followed three years later by the prestigious Cambridge School for Girls.

The children who attended these private schools were only a small fraction of the school population of Cambridge. They came from economically privileged families who were predominantly Yankee, Protestant, and residents of Old Cambridge. Many of these families had powerful financial interests in Cambridge. Therefore it was often said by public school parents that private schools were undemocratic. Actually, there were probably no parents in Cambridge who did not desire the best possible education for their children, but only a small percentage could afford this least self-indulgent of luxuries. Though few families educated their children privately out of social snobbery, the existence of expensive, superior schools underlined the economic and cultural differences within Cambridge. Accordingly, private school education was also a medium of upwards social mobility. A Boston Brahmin complimented a wealthy Cambridge Irishman on his good sense in sending his son to Browne and Nichols and Harvard rather than to Cambridge Latin and Boston University—the Bostonian's way of saying that the young man was almost socially acceptable.

Wealthy, intellectually sophisticated Yankees were not alone in their dissatisfaction with the public schools. Catholics complained that their children had to read the Protestant version of the Bible and recite Protestant prayers. As the schools became more secular, Catholics were further distressed by the lack of moral instruction and religious training available to their youngsters. Parochial schools responded to these concerns, beginning in 1869 with St. Mary's of the Annunciation, which offered education for girls at the rate of one dollar a month, plus extra for lessons in French and music. A Catholic school for boys opened six years later, and there were several more Catholic schools by the end of the century.

Most Cambridge children, however, fell between the expensive private schools and the Catholic institutions. They read, recited, played games, flirted, cheated, and did Swedish gymnastics in public schools; learned sewing, mechanical drawing, Latin, and arithmetic in public schools; played hookey from, hated or worshipped teachers in, flunked subjects in, and carried report cards pridefully or fearfully home from—public schools.

The provincial rivalry among the Port, the Point, and Old Cambridge yielded to the more pressing concerns of a fast-growing city, and by the time 1896 rolled around, Cambridge politicians were congratulating one another on having licked sectionalism forever. This was not all inflationary rhetoric, for two forces had pulled the city closer together than it had been since the Revolution. One of these forces was the Civil War. The other was the temperance movement.

The atmosphere of Cambridge was so antagonistic to organization that it took a genuine crisis to unite its people. As a violent storm causes strangers to become friends, so the Civil War acted upon Cantabrigians. Before the war Cambridge sentiments about slavery were nowhere near unanimous, despite the presence, in Cambridgeport, of the most eloquent of abolitionists, William Lloyd Garrison. The divisions of opinion did not necessarily follow social or ethnic lines. Though James Russell Lowell wittily pleaded the cause of emancipation in his "Biglow Papers"—a satire of the Mexican War as an effort to extend slavery—several Harvard men hesitated to risk the Union for the sake of freeing slaves. Garrison's fiery oratory roused many workingmen, but others considered black an inferior hue and remained unmoved. When war became inevitable, however, Cambridge rallied to defend the Union.

James P. Richardson, great-grandson of Moses Richardson, who died during the British retreat from Lexington in April 1775, anticipated the struggle and began early to organize a corps of volunteers. When the call came from President Lincoln on April 15, 1861, Richardson delivered ninety-five men, and Cambridge produced the first volunteer company in the United States. There were good old Yankee names in the lot, like Cartwright, Nichols, Copps, and Dexter (and Richardson). There were also Celtic names like Gaffney, Kelly, Kennedy, and McCarty. The Irish have already been seen marching from St. John's Literary Institute in East Cambridge to offer their services to the Mayor.

The war aroused Harvard rather less than it did the St. John's Literary Institute. Classes continued without interruption, and it was considered quite acceptable for a young man to hire a person to serve in his place. Lincoln's son was at Harvard until 1864. Nevertheless, over 1,300 current and former Harvard men fought for the Union (and another 257 for the Confederacy), and 40 percent of the class of 1862 enlisted after commencement. When Lee's surrender was announced, the college celebrated by dismissing classes. Students adjourned to the "Delta," where Memorial Hall was later built, for a baseball game.

When the war ended, one sixth of the entire population of Cambridge had served under arms. Three hundred and fifty-two men died. The survivors returned, and Cambridge welcomed them as Cantabrigians—not as Catholics or Protestants, Yankees or foreigners. Lowell, who had lost three nephews and had written the "Commemoration Ode" to honor Harvard's Civil War dead, recited these lines from his poem:

> 'Tis no Man we celebrate,
> By his country's victories great,
> A hero half, and half the whim of Fate,
> But the pith and marrow of a Nation
> Drawing force from all her men,
> Highest, humblest, weakest, all,
> For her time of need, and then
> Pulsing it again through them,
> Till the basest can no longer cower,
> Feeling his soul spring up divinely tall,
> Touched but in passing by her
>   mantle-hem.

The spirit of unity passed its emotional peak and subsided as men resumed less heroic pursuits. Still, it left a residue which made possible that phenomenon called "The Cambridge Idea"—Cambridge's battle with the bottle.

The old YMCA building at Central Square, shown in 1883. It stood until 1926.

Spirits had flowed freely in the town since Puritan days, and Cantabrigians had long overlooked the occasional alcoholic excesses of Harvard undergraduates. Taverns were respectable places where businessmen and others gathered; the Cambridge Humane Society had often convened at Porter's Tavern. Public drunkenness, though frowned upon, was rare and not deemed a social problem. But when Cambridge acquired a large population and a proportionate number of saloons, the street disturbances and barroom brawls began to occur with unsettling frequency. By the 1880s police records showed arrests of more than a thousand drunk and disorderly persons annually.

Temperance was one of those Victorian moral inventions which many Cantabrigians were disposed to embrace. It consisted principally of the theory that alcohol was the prime cause of all the troubles of the laboring classes: poverty, poor health, and loose moral behavior. (How reassuring it must have been to assign complex human conditions to a single cause.) Women, some Harvard professors, and many Old Cambridge Yankees adopted the cause with messianic fervor and formed the Citizens No-License Committee. The Old Cambridge group was epitomized by Frank Foxcroft, the movement's spiritual leader and chief spokesman. He edited the temperance vehicle, *The Frozen Truth*. This group would have achieved little, however, had it not been for the wholehearted support of nearly every clergyman in town. For the first time in Cambridge history, Protestants and Catholics cooperated.

Temperance activists had been busy in Massachusetts since the 1850s. In 1881 the Commonwealth passed a local option law giving the residents of cities and towns the power to vote for "No-License," effectively, to ban bars and saloons within their precincts. No-License was placed on the Cambridge ballot in the same year and lost by a mere six votes. The Citizens No-License Committee, though disappointed by the defeat, felt confident of victory the following year. But local merchants, especially saloon keepers, had been frightened by the narrow margin and started an active counter-campaign using the argument that if people could not get a drink in Cambridge they would take their trade across the river to Boston. In 1882 the pro-saloon votes defeated the No-License votes by 393. Meanwhile, neighboring Somerville passed a No-License law of its own and, much to the delight of Cambridge saloon owners, Somerville men crossed city lines to get their rum.

The saloon votes held their ground for the next three years. The number of saloons in Cambridge rose to 122. "Disorder was on the increase in our streets; those elements which always attend the saloon were becoming dominant at the city hall; and our city fathers were so persuaded of the invulnerable position of the rum power that they considered the city's vote of license as liberty to do the most absurd thing at its behest." So reported the Rev. David Beach.

The vote was finally reversed in 1886, thanks largely to the efforts of Catholic priests who campaigned energetically among their parishioners. Cambridge was thereby purged of saloons and remained officially dry until Prohibition ended in 1933.

After ten years of No-License the temperance leaders congratulated themselves on the fact that the population had increased nearly twice as fast as it did during the saloon era and that, moreover, "the *quality* of the increase has much improved." They claimed credit for rising land valuations and housing starts, increased deposits in savings banks, and "the increased sobriety, industry, skill, and efficiency" among working people. Most of this was balderdash, to borrow from the vocabulary of the day. True, the streets smelt better and were safer for young ladies; and the police arrested one tenth the number of drunks. But Cambridge would have grown and prospered with or without saloons.

The irony of No-License was that Cantabrigians who really wanted a drink had but to walk across the river to a Boston saloon, and one of the reasons why the Cambridge police apprehended so few people for drunkenness was that Boston

FIFTY YEARS A CITY: COMING OF AGE

police did the job instead. Pedestrian traffic on the bridges at night was inclined to rowdiness. Furthermore, the outlawing of saloons inevitably inspired illegal traffic in alcohol within Cambridge. Many a drugstore in the city had a convivial back room where neighborhood regulars could get a drink while someone stood watch for the police. Cambridge lawmen could not keep up with the violations. One of the prominent citizens to recognize the absurdities of the situation was Harvard's president, Charles W. Eliot, who did not share the theories of the temperance movement. He annoyed No-License protagonists by announcing publicly that he did not think the city could enforce the law but said he voted for it anyway because Cambridge had been educated up to the point that it no longer needed a saloon.

Though "The Cambridge Idea" did not eliminate the abuse of alcohol, much less the problems of the poor, it did win a major victory for harmony. Its greatest achievement was the alliance between unlikely elements. The Rev. Mr. Beach said, "Catholics have come to love Protestants, and Protestants to love Catholics." He noted that "Those hateful lines, also, of local jealousy or antagonism between the original nuclei of the city . . . have been largely obliterated, so that we have become one people." Father Thomas Scully, pastor of St. Mary's church on Norfolk Street, joined the refrain. "The saloon seems to have been among us, and you Protestants did not like us Catholics. But now that the saloon is gone, we love one another, and are nobly helpful one toward another." If the clergymen exaggerated, it was the kind of overstatement that the citizens of embattled Cambridge longed to hear.

During the first year of No-License, Cambridge's good godfather, in the person of Frederick Rindge, blessed the newfound harmony. Rindge, a Cambridge boy, had become a rich man in California while

Cambridge City Hall on Massachusetts Avenue at Central Square. The building, completed in 1890, was a gift to the city from Frederick Rindge.

guarding a deep affection for his home town, which he visited frequently. When Mayor William Russell alerted him to Cambridge's need for a public library in 1887, Rindge offered to donate one. A few months later he added a new city hall and a school for industrial training to the list. The Cambridge Public Library and the City Hall still stand and serve their intended purposes; the Manual Training School—the first such public school in the United States—was demolished in 1931 and replaced by the Rindge Technical High School. These structures cost Rindge nearly half a million dollars to build and equip. Asked why he had given them, Rindge explained modestly that he wanted "to establish certain didactic public buildings." He insisted that there be no memorials to him and that his name not be connected with the buildings. (Cambridge could not resist and, after his death, gave his name to Rindge Technical, Rindge Avenue, and Rindge Terrace.) The city was overcome with gratitude. The usual recipient of such generosity was Harvard, not Cambridge.

In fact, Harvard fared excellently during the half century of economic prosperity, In 1896 Byron Hurlbut, Recording Secretary, announced proudly that the combined value of the university's holdings in land, buildings, and money amounted to 13 million dollars. Harvard had sixty buildings, including fifteen dormitories. The university owned or occupied almost 700 acres of land, though over 600 of these were outside Cambridge. (Soldiers Field and the Bussey Institution were in Boston; the biggest single chunk of real estate, the 387-acre Arnold Arboretum, belonged to the City of Boston but was administered by Harvard.) Harvard's total income during the year 1894-95 was $1,084,090—a sum very close to the amount which Cambridge collected in taxes and nearly half the city budget.

Charles W. Eliot (no relation to Indian Bible Eliot of Puritan days) had become university president in 1869. A dynamic man, full of ambition and innovative intelligence, Eliot modernized Harvard. During his forty years in office he reorganized the university; he raised the standards of admission and instruction; he introduced the elective system in the college. Eliot's reforms spread to other institutions of higher learning and filtered down to secondary schools. Harvard achieved the international reputation which it has never lost. (It was also during Eliot's dignified tenure that Harvard's sense of humor burst into print. The Lampoon began its hilarious career in 1876.)

In 1895 Eliot anticipated that the 3,600 students at Harvard might increase three, four, or five times "in centuries to come." (He underestimated slightly; Harvard by 1975 had over 16,000 students, not counting several thousand people taking extension courses in the evenings.) He deliberately added to university properties as a provision for future expansion. Toward the end of the century, when most of Cambridge territory had been built upon, Harvard's acquisitive real estate activities—which were actually quite moderate—provoked some negative comments. People began to notice that Harvard-owned lands were unavailable for business or residential development and did not provide any tax revenue to the city. Eliot countered the objections by pointing to the university's handsome, park-like spaces and promised that "as time goes on," Cambridge would have great reason to be thankful for "the continuing openness of the eighty-two acres which belong to Harvard University"—thus suspending further discussion.

Eliot had a broad concept of universities. He thought that a university, in addition to its direct and obvious purposes, "should exert a unifying social influence. It should set an example of religious toleration, and cultivate mutual respect between diverse churches. A university which draws its students from a large area has also a unifying influence in regard to political discussions and divisions." It is not surprising that a man of such generous attitudes was one of the first people to recognize that Harvard had a responsibility towards the citizens of Cambridge. The university, which had already opened its museum collections for public viewing, increased its schedule of public lectures. Harvard

FIFTY YEARS A CITY: COMING OF AGE

Harvard Square in 1885, showing College House, a dormitory for Harvard students, built by private investors. The building now contains shops, offices, and a movie theatre. Camera points north. At right is the First Parish meeting house (Unitarian), before the steeple was simplified. The horse cars are parked, perhaps waiting for their horses.

grounds lying northeast of the Common, called Jarvis Field, and including a track, a baseball field, and some thirty tennis courts, were made available to the city during the summer recess provided that the city returned them in the fall in the same condition in which they were received. Though the average Cambridge resident of that time did not own a tennis racket and stood in awe of Harvard, these gestures indicated the university's sensitivity to its place within the community.

On the occasion of the city's 50-year birthday celebration in 1896, Eliot chronicled the assets which the presence of Harvard conferred upon Cambridge. They were undeniable: the physical attractiveness of the buildings and grounds, the service of Harvard men on city committees (the School Committee almost always had some Harvard professor in its midst), the level of culture, the gifted and famous people who came to Cambridge for Harvard's sake. Most precious and intangible of all was that "for two hundred and sixty years the lamp of philosophy has been kept burning in this quiet town, and that illumination makes it a brighter place to live in for the present and coming generations."

Cambridge celebrated its first fifty years as a city with the publication of a huge book, *The Cambridge of Eighteen Hundred and Ninety-Six,* in which many authors itemized the city's progress. Cantabrigians knew by then that the town had come of age and was truly an urban place—a very special urban place. Most of the rural vestiges were gone, and the new generations of city dwellers behaved quite differently from their predecessors. "The independence of country life is consistent with a selfishness that is quite out of place in a city," wrote Arthur Gilman wisely in his preface to the memorial volume. "In the crowded town, every man, woman, and child must consider his neighbors." Thus, he continued, "it is necessary in these days to lay deep the foundations of love of city, as distinguished from that love of country which has dominated all true Americans since the moment that Winthrop first set foot on the shores of Newe Towne."

Deliverymen making a stop on Church Street, near Harvard Square, in 1900. Camera points east. At left background is the First Parish meeting house (Unitarian).

8

Finishing Touches

During most of the 1890s, the north side of the Charles remained largely uninspiring. By the beginning of the new century, however, the acres behind the sea wall had been filled with mud dredged from the river bottom. The esplanade—now part of Memorial Drive—was completed and planted with saplings. Yet the Charles River Embankment Company never caught on with prospective buyers, perhaps because the development was so manifestly a suburban island adrift in a sea of tenements, factories, and an unresolved river edge. By 1903 only three structures had been built on the big wedge of property between the river and the railroad. They were the Riverbank Court apartment hotel, the Cambridge City Armory, and the Metropolitan Storage Warehouse, all of which were later acquired by M.I.T.

The potential attractiveness of this section of Cambridgeport did not become obvious until 1910 when, after more than twenty years of argument, proposals, and counter-proposals, the Charles River Dam was completed. The attached houses along Boston's Beacon Street prove how unappealing the old Charles must have been. Built before the dam, Beacon Street houses sit with their backs to the water—a phenomenon which is puzzling until one understands the sequence of landfill, building, and damming. The dam, occupying the site of Andrew Craigie's Canal Bridge, brought about the single greatest cosmetic change in Cambridge history. The marshes and mudflats vanished forever. (So, too, did the oyster beds, but with pollution causing objectional stenches, Charles River oysters must have been hazardous victuals.)

The lower river became a wide majestic lake of brackish water, permanently fixed at a level nine feet above mean low tide and linked to the sea by a set of locks for pleasure craft. Sailboats and racing shells on this Charles River Basin replaced the coal and lumber barges of the nineteenth century. Cambridge protected the river edge from industrial sprawl by developing the shoreline park advised by the landscape architects. Upstream from the Basin the river became a gleaming, curvaceous waterway held within definite boundaries and gradually shedding the coal yards, warehouses, docks, gas-works and other industrial installations that had littered its banks even up to and beyond Harvard University.

As the city was going through the last phases of topographical facelift, the Massachusetts Institute of Technology—in those days often called "Boston Tech"—was considering new quarters. By 1902 it had overgrown the six acres which it occupied near Copley Square in Boston and was casting about for a building site. President Eliot of Harvard, who had once taught chemistry at Tech, had tried for many years to lure the Institute into a merger, but M.I.T. rebuffed all efforts at amalgamation and insisted on its independence. Harvard, having failed to absorb M.I.T., now dangled a tantalizing piece of real estate in Allston, adjoining Soldiers Field where the first reinforced concrete stadium in this country was at that moment rising. M.I.T. turned down the offer as though in fear of being overwhelmed by proximity to the older, richer, more powerful institution.

The last year of Eliot's presidency, 1909, coincided with the inauguration of a new M.I.T. president, Richard C. Maclaurin. Maclaurin dined with an M.I.T. alumnus in Boston who, from his rear window on Beacon Street, gestured toward the open land across the river, that area which the Charles River Embankment Company had hoped to develop as residential property. The site had already been considered and rejected by M.I.T. trustees, and Maclaurin's host itemized an intimidating list of objections to it. Nevertheless, Maclaurin was impressed by the location. Word went

The lower Charles — two scenes as Cambridge puts its river bank into shape. TOP: Dredge takes mud from river bottom and pumps it over the new sea wall to fill in the wetlands where Memorial Drive now runs. BOTTOM: Harvard Bridge soon after its 1890 completion. Boston is in background. That part of Massachusetts Avenue in foreground was then only a causeway over the wetlands. M.I.T.'s early buildings were constructed on filled land to left of causeway between the river and the railroad.

FINISHING TOUCHES

The upper Charles — two scenes of the tidal river before it was dammed in 1910. TOP: Looking eastward along Mount Auburn Street at low tide. On horizon, just left of center, is the spire of the First Parish meeting house at Harvard Square. Farther to left is the bulky tower of Memorial Hall. BOTTOM: Enjoying the water at Captain's Island, off the foot of Magazine Street, in 1899. The island now is part of the mainland. The area is known as Magazine Beach. When pollution put the Charles off limits to bathers, a swimming pool was built there.

around that he fancied Cambridge.

A. Lawrence Lowell succeeded Eliot at Harvard. In June 1910 Harvard awarded Maclaurin an LL.D. degree, an honor possibly intended to soften the blow that fell in July when Lowell told Maclaurin flatly that Harvard opposed M.I.T.'s move across the river. The Harvard Corporation, Lowell wrote, was "strongly of opinion that it would be a very serious peril to both institutions to have the Institute of Technology establish itself in Cambridge." The Corporation's objection was quite precise: university officials were concerned that the arrival of M.I.T. would precipitate discussions on the question of tax-exempt lands within Cambridge, and Harvard had no desire to risk the loss of its tax-free status.

Somewhat resentful of Harvard's cold shoulder, Maclaurin looked for alternatives—always carefully bypassing the site next to Soldiers Field which Harvard persisted in pressing. He encountered financial difficulties and, in a despairing mood, remarked to a journalist that "Technology might have to pull up stakes and move to some place where the cost of living is within its means." His comment was repeated in the newspapers, prompting a number of invitations from other Massachusetts towns. Even the Chicago *Evening Post* observed that "we could support a 'Boston Tech' with our loose change, and we wouldn't, like some cities we know of, have to search all the hinterland roundabout to find the money."

Challenged, Cambridge came to life. The Citizens' Trade Association, the Cambridge Club, the Economy Club, the Taxpayers' Association and, most significant, the City Council and the Mayor issued invitations for M.I.T. to come to Cambridge and pooh-poohed the tax problem. The Council's action followed an evening of denunciation of Harvard and its tax-exempt status. As Harvard stood to share in any tax concessions offered to M.I.T., Lowell dropped his arguments. In 1911 and 1912, Maclaurin succeeded in attracting financial support from the Commonwealth of Massachusetts plus a $2,500,000 gift from George Eastman, founder and president of the Eastman Kodak Company, who requested that his contribution be kept anonymous. "May I tell my wife?" Maclaurin asked. "Well, yes, but no one else," replied Eastman. His gift was announced under the name of "Smith."

M.I.T. negotiated thirty-five separate transactions to acquire forty-three acres of land east of the Harvard Bridge, between the railroad tracks and the river. Welles Bosworth, an alumnus, was retained as architect of the new campus. He produced a dignified neoclassical complex crowned by a monumental dome and consistent with the popular architectural tastes of the era. The first completed building on the site was a temporary structure to house the aerodynamics laboratory. On a fine fall day in 1916, M.I.T. moved ceremoniously from Boston. The president and trustees floated across the river on an ornate barge, the *Bucentaur,* which would have been worthy of Cleopatra.

While M.I.T. was buying up Cambridge riverfront properties, workmen were busy digging a subway between Park Street in Boston and Harvard Square. The construction took almost three years and was completed in March 1912. The subway emerged from subterranean Boston, crossed the Charles via the Cambridge Bridge (built between 1900 and 1906 in place of the West Boston Bridge and now called the Longfellow Bridge) and burrowed beneath Cambridge, stopping at Kendall and Central squares en route to the terminus at Harvard Square where passengers could make connections with trolley lines to the north and west.

Having narrowly missed acquiring a steel elevated railway along the same route, Cambridge was generally enthusiastic about the new $10 million rapid transit line which cut commuting time between Harvard Square and Boston to eight minutes. The subway did not affect the distribution or size of Cambridge population; street railways had set those trends half a century earlier. But commercial activity picked up around every subway stop, particularly at Harvard Square, the principal transportation interchange. A pretentious subway station—in the Greek style, of no architec-

FINISHING TOUCHES

The Charles River basin in 1976. Beyond the sailboat is M.I.T.'s 22-story Center for Earth Sciences, built in 1964.

Bucentaur, the ceremonial barge that brought M.I.T. from Boston to Cambridge in 1916. Here you see its launching at Manchester, Massachusetts.

Bird's-eye drawing of electric streetcars in Harvard Square in 1906. You are looking toward Harvard Yard.

tural merit—dominated the center of the Square until 1928 when it was replaced by the current structure which, in the words of a member of the Cambridge Historical Commission, "looks like a trailer stranded in the middle of Massachusetts Avenue."

In October 1912, seven months after the subway was completed, "Stadium Station" opened. The subway line continued underground from Harvard Square and carried passengers almost to the corner of Boylston Street and Charles River Road—now Memorial Drive. From there it was just a short walk across the bridge to the Harvard stadium. The Harvard football team was the undefeated national champion that year, as it had been in 1910, and would be again in 1913 and 1919. Stadium Station was used on football Saturdays until 1959. The site, where the maintenance shops for subway trains and the carhouse for streetcars and trackless trolleys were also located, nearly became the home of the John F. Kennedy Library.

The new subway made a very deep impression on one Harvard freshman, Buckminster Fuller. Four generations of Fuller men had preceded Buckminster at Harvard, and he had read their reminiscences telling of day-long trips driving or walking from Cambridge to Boston across the Great Bridge. Fuller felt intuitively that the subway "was harbinger of an entirely new distance-time relationship of humanity and its transforming environment," and thus this mundane form of transportation helped form the imagination of one of the century's most original thinkers.

Harvard, like Cambridge, achieved mature physical form during the early decades of the twentieth century. This was largely the work of President Lowell, who, with ambition and sense of order, oversaw more construction than all Harvard presidents before him combined. A series of structures along Massachusetts Avenue enclosed Harvard Yard and gave it spatial continuity while screening out the commercial affairs of Harvard Square. Among the buildings of the Lowell administration (1909-1933): Widener Library, the Biological Laboratories, Paine Hall, Lehman Hall, the Fogg Museum, Straus Hall—there was so much building activity at Harvard that

FINISHING TOUCHES

Digging the subway at Harvard Square in May 1910. The subway opened in March 1912. Frame building at top is Harvard's Wadsworth House.

The first subway kiosk in Harvard Square. You are looking east along Massachusetts Avenue in the 1920s. This ornate station was taken down in 1928.

the grounds sometimes looked like a bomb target.

The university's land acquisitions during this period were sizable. Harvard expansion south of Massachusetts Avenue down towards the Charles dates from the Lowell era as do Eliot House, Lowell House, and the other handsome university residences that adorn the riverside. Small wonder that M.I.T.'s designs on Cambridge had caused consternation at Harvard. And sure enough, M.I.T. began consuming new lands west of Massachusetts Avenue in 1924. City officials, seeing prime real estate fall from the tax rolls like autumn leaves, began to fidget. Four years later, Cambridge, Harvard, and M.I.T. reached the agreement—still in force in a slightly updated form—by which each university pays the city an annual lump sum in lieu of taxes.

In 1910 Daniel Crowley and his wife, Mary, had their sixth child. At that time they were living in a cold-water flat on the corner of Webster Avenue and Seckel Street, midway between Inman Square and East Cambridge. Crowley had started life on a tenant farm in County Cork, Ireland, in 1872. Twenty years later—at a time when Irish immigration to the United States had fallen off—his aunt sent him the fare to come to America. Crowley purchased space in steerage and landed in Boston. He found a job at the Barbour-Stockwell Foundry near Kendall Square, settled in Cambridge, and in 1896, when the city was celebrating its semi-centennial, Crowley married Mary Ryan, an Irish-American girl who cooked for a family in Boston's Back Bay. She left her employment to raise their family. They named their sixth child Charles, and

Two oarsmen on the Charles, photographed through an arch on Larz Anderson Bridge. In the background are the Weeks foot bridge and Harvard's Dunster House.

FINISHING TOUCHES

Subway trains and streetcars must have power stations, repair shops, and storage yards. This photograph was taken May 1, 1929, from 1,000 feet up. From the Charles you are looking north-northeast up Boylston Street toward Harvard Square near the top. At right is the Harvard Power Station of the Boston Elevated Railway Company, about to be replaced by Harvard's Eliot House. At center: the Eliot Square Shops and tracks full of subway cars. Adjacent to Boylston Street is the platform of what was then "Stadium Station." At left: the Bennett Street Carhouse, with about 75 streetcars in sight. The subway and car facilities were to have been replaced by the Kennedy Library; the plan was abandoned in 1975 but the facilities were doomed anyhow.

Charles Crowley's upbringing was a good deal like that of many other second-generation immigrants in Cambridge.

It was a polyglot neighborhood. The Crowleys' tenant-landlord was Polish, and there were Irish, Russians, Italians, Jews from Eastern Europe, and families that had been American for generations living within a few blocks of one another. Charlie grew up with the aroma of blintzes in the air and believing that two pieces of bread with something in between them were called a "sendvich." He knew how ravioli and stuffed cabbage tasted, and his vocabulary was spiced with words of many languages. He attended St. Mary's grammar school. In summer his father took him to baseball games between the Barbour-Stockwell team and one of the other factory teams. In the fall and winter, Charlie and his friends foraged for wood down behind the City Armory on Massachusetts Avenue at Vassar Street. Charlie went on to public high school. His family moved to a better house in 1926. Crowley was a student at Boston College for one year during the Depression, usually walking all the way to the campus to save on carfare. He quit college for lack of funds and joined the Cambridge Fire Department.

By 1910 when Charlie was born, Cambridge population showed no signs of leveling off. There were fewer Irish immigrants but many Swedes, Russians, Portuguese, Poles, Armenians, Italians, Greeks, Slavs, and other European peoples whose numbers were too small to arouse the statistical interest of census takers. Like the Irish before them, the new immigrants were often poor and unskilled. They looked upon America—and Cambridge—as the promised land.

Not all the immigrants came to stay. A number of Greeks, for example, planned to make their fortunes in America and return to Greece. More often than not, however, the making of fortunes took longer than anticipated. Many Greeks never went back to the old country. Some did, and therefore one can find English-speaking individuals in unlikely corners of Greece, in some island village or on a few acres of rocky ancestral farm on the Peloponnesos. They

The Immigrant Boy, a symbol of one of the epics of American and Cambridge history. This old photograph by Charles Henry Currier is in the Library of Congress. The boy is said to be an Italian arrival in Boston. Think of him as representative of the Irish, Greeks, Italians, Portuguese, and others who made new lives in America.

live comfortably, sometimes on Social Security checks, which go further in Greece than they do in Cambridge. Ask and they will tell you of their years in the United States and pull out photographs of their children who are American citizens.

One of the many Greeks who stayed in Cambridge was Felix Caragianes, an example of a poor immigrant who prospered in the new surroundings. He left a small Peloponnesian town called Megalopolis around the turn of the century and arrived in America with one dollar in his pocket. He got a job in a shoe factory in Lynn, Massachusetts, and then started shining shoes in Cambridge and saving his pennies. Eventually he opened a shoe-repair and hat-cleaning shop in Harvard Square. Its green awning with "Felix" on it was a Harvard landmark for decades. At one time Caragianes owned valuable real estate in the Square. He lived in a large house on Garfield Street and made his own wine in the basement. His kitchen was a meeting place for his Greek relatives and friends. He had never been to school, even in Greece, and he never did learn to read and write English, but he had a reverence for education, loved Harvard professors and students alike, and helped many a student through Harvard. For Caragianes, town and gown were hand in glove.

While foreign parents struggled with the vagaries of the English language, their children went to school and learned to speak like native Americans. Whereas Boston had large districts packed solidly with Irish or Italians, Cambridge neighborhoods were more heterogeneous. There were some observable patterns: Portuguese, Poles, Armenians, and Italians tended to settle among the Irish in East Cambridge. The blacks gravitated toward Cambridgeport. But the most common pattern was mixture—Yankees, immigrants, Irish-Americans—all within a few blocks or a few houses of each other. Cambridge might have been the stage set for Israel Zangwill's play, *The Melting Pot*, which introduced the concept and the phrase into the popular vocabulary in 1909.

Except that Cambridge was more like a salad. Though tossed together, the cucumbers, peppers, onions, tomatoes, radishes, and lettuce retained their characteristic flavor and texture. Old country customs and traditions passed from one generation to another along with grandmother's recipes and the melody of a lullaby. Everybody loved baseball, but the Portuguese still played soccer, and the Italians got together for *bocce*, or bowling. Separate places of worship and social clubs, both in Cambridge and in Boston, kept the individual cultural traditions alive. Instead of attending the existing Catholic churches in East Cambridge, the Polish people went over to Boston until 1905 when they bought the old Universalist church—which had fallen on hard times because of the decline in the number of Protestants in East Cambridge—and renovated it for their own uses. The basement became a Polish social center and served as a meeting place for the Polish political club, two women's societies, and two charitable organizations.

The fact that people of widely different backgrounds shared close quarters in no way guaranteed happy relations among them. Fierce competition among poor people generated myths and damaging preconceptions about the intellectual capabilities or the moral fitness of different ethnic groups. Jews who fled the *pogroms* of Russia and moved into the poorest Irish districts in Cambridgeport received a rough welcome in America. Neighborhood children harassed Jewish youngsters on the way to school, and for a while it was physically dangerous for Jews to walk on certain streets. Failing to receive adequate protection from Cambridge police, Jews formed their own protective organization and succeeded in eliminating the violence—though not the prejudice.

Blacks suffered the most crippling forms of discrimination. Between 1875 and 1910 the Negro community grew from 921 to 3,500. Because the color of their skin set them apart from all other members of the community, they gathered in tight districts in Cambridgeport. Those who could afford better quarters lived around Howard Street; the more usual residences were rickety old shacks on former marshland down by the Charles. Most blacks worked in Boston in menial jobs. Cambridge industries would not hire them for fear of stirring up trouble among the white factory laborers, who were overwhelmingly opposed to working beside blacks. Thus, although black parents usually sent their children to grammar school, they often discouraged them from finishing high school or learning special skills because there were so few opportunities to apply education.

A black man would have had an easier time getting into Harvard than obtaining a job in the factory which employed Charles Crowley's father. Harvard had accepted Negroes since the Civil War. Clement Morgan, the first black ever elected to the

A noon class for immigrants at the Cambridge YMCA at Central Square. The blackboard indicates that these are workers from John P. Squire & Company (see picture of plant on page 64).

The Cambridge Recreation Department arranged sports activities throughout the city. Here, girls' teams compete in a league game at Thorndike Field, East Cambridge, in the 1920s.

FINISHING TOUCHES

Cambridge Board of Aldermen (in 1896), had graduated from Harvard College and the Harvard Law School. Black Harvard students were extremely few, but they ate in Memorial Hall, slept in the dormitories, and kept some Southern whites from applying. There were also Jews and Irish Catholics at Harvard, but college education, at Harvard or anywhere else, was still a great luxury, and scholarships were much scarcer than they are today.

While new immigrant groups were struggling to gain a foothold in Cambridge, the Irish of the first and second generations—those folk whom John F. Kennedy once slyly called "the oppressed majority"—realized their political potential. In 1901 Cambridge elected its first Irish Mayor, one John H. H. McNamee, a man with sure political instincts and the gift of blarney, who defeated the incumbent David T. Dickinson, Republican and Yankee. The Irish went on to dominate Cambridge politics for nearly four decades. If the Mayor was not an Irishman, at least the Irish captured a majority of City Council seats and administrative posts within the city.

Thomas P. O'Neill, Sr., father of U.S. Representative Thomas P. "Tip" O'Neill, was a classic Irish politician. Raised as a bricklayer in North Cambridge, O'Neill Sr. was a popular, clever man whose first school of politics was the labor union. In 1900 his ward sent him to the City Council; in 1914 he scored the highest mark on a civil service exam for the job of Superintendent of Sewers in Cambridge. This position and marriage to the daughter of an executive of the Edison Cambridge Gaslight Company put O'Neill in control of a great number of jobs. "In North Cambridge, he became known as 'The Governor,'" wrote Jimmy Breslin in *How the Good Guys Finally Won*. "He ran the North Cambridge Knights of Columbus baseball team, was President of St. John's Holy Name Society and—strict Irish rather than dreaming Irish—head of the St. Matthew's Temperance Society. Nobody in his house was allowed to wear anything that did not have a union label on it." Breslin further delights in telling that on the day "Tip" was born, O'Neill Sr. was picketing Harvard with representatives from the bricklayers' union. If a politician wanted the North Cambridge Irish vote, he was well advised to solicit O'Neill's help. The old man had Tip out on the streets ringing doorbells at the age of fifteen.

The Yankee professionals and businessmen who had run Cambridge during the nineteenth century, disheartened by the rising tide of Irish, backed off from politics and civil service, leaving the way open for Democratic-run machine politics. Tax rates crept up, but as long as industry boomed and Cambridge acquired such improvements as the Charles River Dam, the park system, and the subway, Cantabrigians accepted government by the Irish. Factories poured into Cambridge one after another: Simplex Wire and Cable on Sidney Street; Lamb & Ritchie (sheet metal) on Albany Street; Johnson-Appleby (jams) on Memorial Drive. In 1913 Henry Ford built an automobile assembly plant at 640 Memorial Drive. These were only some of the many manufacturers who determined that Cambridge was a hospitable location.

A few anxious voices were raised—not about the Irish but about the course of growth in general. Samuel Atkins Eliot noted in 1913 that "there is but little vacant land now left in Cambridge and in some parts of the city there is already dangerous congestion. As the population multiplies, the city must see to it that the buildings which are erected for dwelling purposes are suitable for people to live in. Cambridge must prevent the growth of slums ... The time has gone by when the industrial preeminence of a city was crudely judged by the volumes of smoke pouring from the factory chimneys ... These are now recognized as nuisances that no progressive city will tolerate." Most people did not pay much attention to Eliot's words, and even those that did soon became distracted by more compelling events.

The United States did not enter the First World War as an active combatant until 1917. When President Wilson signed the declaration of war on April 6, Cambridge was ready—as Cambridge had always been ready in national emergencies. Over 8,000 young men, representing every part of Cambridge from Brattle Street to Bridge Street, became soldiers. Harvard students were as keen to do battle as any fighting Irishman. Before the United States declared war, the university offered a course entitled "Military Science I," and had a Reserve Officers' Training Corps. Students enlisted in flocks. After the summer of 1918, when the federal government put all college students into uniform, every Harvard student who was not near-sighted or flat-footed (as the historian Samuel Eliot Morison put it) was a soldier.

The government established a Naval Radio School in two Harvard buildings shortly after the United States entered the war. Within six months, this school had taken over most of the university buildings north of Harvard Yard, including Memorial Hall. Military barracks covered the Cambridge Common. Down river, M.I.T. had no chance to ease into a normal routine in its new home. Army and Navy men swarmed over the site, and the place looked more like a mobilization camp than a university. The young Vannevar Bush of M.I.T. shared his research on underwater sound detection with the War Department.

Cambridge industry expanded eagerly in response to the special demands which the war effort created. By the end of the war, Cambridge ranked as the second industrial city in Massachusetts, and the combined value of industrial products had jumped from $50 million in 1910 to over $100 million.

The war naturally took precedence over civic affairs. Cantabrigians shared patriotic sentiments, and there was, perhaps, a greater solidarity within the city than was usually in evidence. But since the old sectional rivalries had lost their edge anyway and the new divisions had not yet assumed articulate forms, wartime unity did not amount to much. When the armistice was announced, Cambridge rejoiced with parades and speeches and tried to slide back into a familiar groove.

Surface appearances were normal. Though the population growth rate subsided and immigration dropped off sharply during the 1920s because of federal quotas, Cambridge had 113,643 residents by 1930. Industry continued to record impressive gains during the twenties. Nearly every square foot of buildable land in the city—including that which had been created along the banks of the Charles River—was occupied. Apartment houses of four, five, and six stories began to pop up among the old two-story and three-story buildings. Automobiles displaced horses on Cambridge streets and—as there were ample parking spaces and no real traffic problems—every man dreamed of owning his own car. Harvard enrollment (including graduate and professional schools) stood at over 5,000 in 1930, and M.I.T. was also rapidly multiplying.

But people no longer acclaimed growth with unqualified approval. The war had damaged the myth of progress. The words of Samuel Atkins Eliot and others interested in city planning began to acquire urgency. City Hall made vague gestures in the direction of controlling subsequent growth: the revised building code of 1924 incorporated Cambridge's first zoning law. The Planning Board, which had been handicapped by a lack of financing and a purely advisory role since its inception in 1913, showed vital signs and prepared a number of studies on topics such as riverfront development, tree-planting, zoning, and traffic.

The habit of unrestricted growth was hard to conquer, however. Cambridge's zoning laws and planning boards of the 1920s had more symbolic than real value. If nothing else, they indicated a concern with what the city had become and an apprehension of what it might be in the future if it continued, like Topsy, to just grow.

9

New Directions

The 1920s terminated in an international financial debacle which made the little crises that preceded it unworthy of the word "depression," and it was on that cheerless note that Cambridge graduated into its fourth century. The next ten years were some of the grimmest (and, paradoxically, wackiest) in Cambridge history. For the first time since the seventeenth century when Thomas Hooker decamped with his flock, Cambridge actually lost population; between 1930 and 1940 Cantabrigians decreased by 4 percent. This did not make Cambridge a freak. The same pattern was repeated in cities like Boston, Philadelphia, and Cleveland. But Cambridge had other troubles. Assessed property valuations dropped from $191,237,400 in 1932 to $170,603,600 in 1940 while the tax rate was rising from $37.20 per thousand to $43. In view of the present tax rates, it seems odd that $43 could cause a commotion, but businessmen, property owners, and bankers got very edgy during the thirties. Moreover, the city fell further and further into debt.

Harvard celebrated its three hundredth birthday in the midst of Cambridge gloom in 1936. The university staged the "Harvard Tercentenary Conference of Arts and Sciences," a two-week congregation of 2,700 scholars who heard lectures by such luminaries as Jean Piaget, Karl Jung, Howard Mumford Jones, Alfred North Whitehead, John Dewey, Albert Einstein, John Enders, and J. Robert Oppenheimer—to list only a few of the dazzling names. Sir Arthur Stanley Eddington spoke about "The Cosmical Constant and the Recession of the Nebulae," and Werner Jaeger discussed "The Problem of Authority and the Crisis of the Greek Spirit."

Illuminating though it was for Harvard men, the Tercentenary celebration did not comfort Cambridge in its civic misery. Industry and commerce suffered every hike in the tax rate with pain. Cambridge acquired the reputation of being one of the worst-run cities in Massachusetts. More and more, disgruntled taxpayers blamed their woes on fiscal mismanagement by the Irish-Americans who controlled City Hall, but the prospects of dislodging the incumbent politicians seemed non-existent.

Then, in 1938, and partly on the urging of influential Cambridge citizens, the Massachusetts General Court approved "Plan E" as a local-option form of city charter. Cambridge had been operating since 1924 under a modified "Plan B" form of government: a City Council of fifteen (eleven elected from the city's eleven wards and four at large) plus an elected Mayor. Plan E, a variation on Council-Manager government, provides for a Council of nine elected at large by *Proportional Representation*. The Council then selects a Mayor from its membership. The Mayor presides over meetings of the Council and the School Committee and performs in ceremonial roles but has no executive power. Instead, the chief administrative officer of the city is a City Manager appointed by the majority of the Council. The Manager serves at the Council's pleasure and may be discharged at any time.

The tricky part of Plan E is Proportional Representation, a voting system popular with political reformers at the turn of the century and, at the time it came up in Cambridge, already in use in New York and Cincinnati. Candidates for City Council and School Committee run at large. Each voter ranks them by preference by marking 1, 2, 3, and so on after their names on the ballot. This preferential voting leads to the two basic features of Proportional Representation which distinguish it from the commonly used plurality system (where a voter marks his ballot with X's for as many candidates as there are seats to be filled). First, each ballot counts for only one candidate—usually the No. 1 choice—but a ballot will be reassigned to the next lower

Counting the votes for Cambridge City Council in 1971, in the gymnasium of Longfellow School on Broadway. The process goes on for days.

preferred candidate if the No. 1 choice has more votes than needed to win or too few to stay in the running. And second, a winning candidate need receive only a fraction of the votes cast (roughly, the total vote divided by the number of the seats to be filled). The time needed to reassign ballots means that Cambridge waits days to find out who has been elected. Cantabrigians go over to the Longfellow School to watch the election clerks walking from one pile of votes to another.

Proportional Representation, or PR, is, as its name implies, a way to give each group of like-minded voters representation in proportion to its voting strength. Ideally it gives the majority control with minority representation and results in elective bodies which are a cross-section of the electorate. Thus PR offered Cambridge reformers, who had lost a voice in city government, an opportunity to be heard. The Council-Manager arrangement was an effort to cleanse city government by depoliticizing the administrative officer and making him accountable to the elected Councillors.

Plan E had been advocated in Cambridge years earlier by Harvard professor Lewis Jerome Johnson. When the General Court authorized the Plan E option in 1938, the professor's son, Chandler W. Johnson, a Cambridge resident, took the lead in organizing "The Cambridge Committee for Plan E." The group comprised frustrated businessmen, many other taxpayers, and representatives of the League of Women Voters. Initially the members were people who lived in the handsome residential areas west of Harvard Square. After a brief internal struggle between conservative and liberal elements, the committee offered the chairmanship to James W. Landis, dean of the Harvard Law School and a New Deal Democrat with close connections to Franklin D. Roosevelt. It was assumed that Landis's prominence as a Democrat would offset the possible disadvantages of his Harvard ties, and that his name was well enough known to get publicity in Boston newspapers. Landis accepted the position, built a vigorous campaign organization, and distributed responsible roles among representatives of different religious and ethnic groups.

The Plan E committee's immediate objective was to collect sufficient signatures for a referendum in order to have the Plan E option appear on the ballot in November 1938. Volunteers, particularly from the League of Women Voters, succeeded in obtaining the necessary number and filed the petitions in October with the City Council, which, in turn, was supposed to forward them to the Massachusetts Secretary of State. This the Councillors deliberately neglected to do, and the Plan E committee had to resort to legal action. Cambridge politics began to assume comic-opera qualities. The deadline for transmission happened to be a Saturday, and Council members headed for the Harvard Stadium to see the football game, according to the custom by which the university endows Cambridge Councillors with complimentary season tickets. As each Councillor arrived at his seat he was greeted by a deputy holding a summons requiring the immediate holding of a Council meeting.

The maneuver succeeded, and the petitions reached the State House just before the deadline expired. But the incident caused Dean Landis to lose his temper and good judgment. Over the phone from Washington, he called the Cambridge City Council "a cheap gang of politicians." It was a costly tactical blunder. Thomas M. McNamara, the Council president, responded indelicately with: "Cultured shysters have resorted to the lowest form of campaigning." Councillors, who had up to that point been rather passive, mobilized against Plan E and labeled it a Harvard plot. Councillor John J. Toomey hastily formed the "People's Committee for the Preservation of Democracy in Cambridge," charged that Plan E was a device of "Harvard communists," and then proceeded to introduce a motion calling upon Massachusetts to take necessary steps to make Harvard a separate city.

Such shenanigans made bright newspaper copy, and the Plan E campaign received coverage far beyond Cambridge borders. The *New York Times* of October 19, 1938, ran a headline reading: VOTE TO SECEDE FROM HARVARD IS TAKEN BY CAMBRIDGE CITY COUNCIL. Two days later the irrepressible Harvard *Lampoon* got into the act by sending an ultimatum to City Council demanding that "a buffer state be set up between Harvard and the Cambridge City Hall and its boundaries be defined by a neutral commission headed by former Governor Curley" and that "the Harvard Lampoon be made a free city."

Lampooners followed up their demands the next day with a mock storm trooper march down Massachusetts Avenue—minus a parade permit. As the marchers approached City Hall, Councillor Michael (Mickey the Dude) Sullivan was descending the steps. He confronted the students and tried to stop the parade. Some sort of scuffle ensued, and Sullivan fell—probably accidentally. However, Sullivan tumbled in front of a news photographer who took a picture which gave the impression that the Councillor had been kicked by a Harvard student in jackboots. The picture ran in most of the Boston newspapers and damaged the Plan E campaign. Landis was furious and descended upon Lampoon headquarters to chew out the editors.

The City Councillors used their influence among the 2,600 city employees, who represented one of the largest voting blocks in Cambridge. The People's Committee ran advertisements quoting Al Smith (a hero in heavily Democratic, Roman Catholic Cambridge) thus: "Of all the wild-eyed crazy nonsensical things that have ever afflicted the City of New York, there is nothing that equals proportional representation." When the Cambridge Communist Party started circulating anti-Plan E pamphlets advising that PR was anti-labor and anti-democratic, the People's Committee switched their line from Harvard-communist-plot to fascist-plot and talked about weighted ballots in Austria and Germany. When the 1938 election day arrived, Cambridge voters rejected Plan E by a narrow margin.

Mayor John L. Lyons's second term got off to a poor start. He submitted a budget proposing a 10 percent boost in city expenditures, a raise which would have required an increase of $5 or maybe $7 in the tax rate. Since the budget was presented in summary form instead of in the itemized version stipulated by law, Lyons's opponents—a citizen group working with the Taxpayers' Association and Plan E advocates—took the budget to court where it was declared to be illegal. Cambridge was thereby obliged to operate on the budget for the previous year. Lyons was in a bad position, because he had already expanded the city payrolls; also, the city was already perilously close to its debt ceiling.

The 1940 tax rate of $43 per thousand gave Cambridge the distinction of having very nearly the highest in Massachusetts; nearly $10 of the $43 was required to pay interest on the city's debt. Valuations had dropped another $1.2 million during the year as industry continued to desert the city. Still more businesses would have liked to relocate but could not afford to because of their heavy capital investments in Cambridge. With the situation deteriorating rapidly, the Plan E committee regrouped early in preparation for a new campaign. In August of 1940 they heard an encouraging rumor: the District Attorney had opened an investigation into the manner in which City Hall hired trucks and other city services.

The 1940 Plan E campaign was more subdued than the 1938 fight. The silliness went out of the contest. Scared by the close-

Central Square in the 1930s. Camera points northwest along Massachusetts Avenue. The ten-story white building at left, a block and a half away, is the Central Square Building in the heart of the Square. It was erected in 1926 and was Cambridge's first "skyscraper." Across the avenue and two blocks farther is the tower of City Hall.

ness of the 1938 vote, the Councillors deliberately remained quiet, each hoping to be elected under the new system should it win. The only person certain to lose his job under Plan E was Mayor Lyons, and so it was Lyons who carried on the fight from City Hall. He sent personal letters to all city employees urging them to work against the plan. Harvard stopped being an issue. Opponents of Plan E attacked PR instead, claiming that it encouraged voting along group and racial lines and that it was undemocratic because it elevated minorities to majorities.

Advocates of Plan E campaigned energetically, reaching out to local clubs and soliciting endorsements from Catholic and ethnic leaders, as the temperance advocates had done during the nineteenth century.

In November 1940, Cambridge voters adopted Plan E by a majority of 59 percent. Plan E won in eight of the eleven city wards, losing as expected in East and North Cambridge, which were heavily Irish, Democratic, and anti-Harvard. (Registered Democrats outnumbered Republicans in East Cambridge 25 to 1.) Not surprisingly, Plan E got its biggest vote from the wards closest to Harvard Square. But a 59 percent majority meant that the reform movement had won broad support. People were not necessarily enamored of Plan E—many who voted for it could not explain how PR worked—but they were fed up with the government they had.

As a Plan E government was not scheduled to take office until January 1942, Cambridge endured a lame duck administration for more than a year. Meanwhile Mayor Lyons got into deeper and deeper trouble. In January 1941 he was indicted on sixty-four counts involving fee-splitting; he posted $2,500 bail and continued in office. Asked by the Council to request an appropriation for new snow plows, Lyons refused saying "the Almighty sends the snow . . . He will in time remove it." The remark appeared in newspapers as far away as London. At the next Council meeting, the Chief of Police reported that four of the nine police cars belonging to the city were propped up on boxes in the police station and had been stripped to supply spare parts to keep the other five on the road. Quoth the Chief: "The cars are no good to chase anyone. They couldn't catch another car." Then came the Mayor's conviction in mid-March on forty-two counts of requesting and accepting bribes. This compelled him to relinquish his office, and Cambridge limped along with an acting mayor until January 1942 when Plan E went into effect.

The first Council of nine members under the new system had only four who had been endorsed by the Plan E reformers. Among them were John H. Corcoran, partner in Cambridge's first big successful Irish-American business venture, which his father had started, and Edward A. Crane, another Irish-American Democrat with a talent for pleasing both political camps. Corcoran became the first Plan E Mayor. Crane, son of a Cambridge policeman and Harvard '35, became Mayor in 1950 for one term and later held the office for three consecutive terms from 1960 to 1966; he was the only Cambridge politician of his time to have been described as a "mover and shaker." Though the Plan E group was disappointed not to have captured the majority of seats on the Council of 1942, the other five Councillors could seldom get together and reform policies therefore dominated.

For their City Manager the 1942 Council chose Colonel John B. Atkinson, a veteran of World War I and a prominent international shoe salesman, born and raised in Cambridge. Although he had never run a city, he had managed a successful business, and he was a strong personality, determined to perform his duties without reference to factional politics. He did not depend on his Manager's salary for his livelihood and did not fear losing his job. The amount of favorable publicity he received did not endear him to Council members, nor did his inclination to assume power without their consent. "Mickey the Dude" Sullivan, who had hated Plan E from the beginning and did not like it any more when he was elected under it, habitually referred to Atkinson during Council debates as a "$15-a-week clerk." But Atkinson kept his job for ten years until ousted in a surprise coup. Harvard awarded him an honorary degree in 1951.

Council–Manager government—or, as it operated during Atkinson's term in office, Manager–Council government—achieved what it had been elected to do. Cambridge was the only city in Massachusetts to reduce its tax rate each year from 1942 to 1947. Despite a reduction in city work hours, basic salary increases averaging more than fifty percent, and postwar inflation, the 1950 tax rate was $6.60 less than the 1941 rate. At the same time, municipal services improved a lot. The Police Department now owned sixteen cruisers, either brand-new or in prime condition. The Public Works Department had thirty-five snow plows to remove what the Almighty sent. Street construction costs plunged from an average cost per mile of $51,989 in 1941 to $14,271 in 1949 because the city had purchased equipment instead of contracting out the work.

Any honest and well-run city government, Plan E or not, could have done as much. Boston, which had a similar situation and similar voting patterns, made a reform of sorts in the late 1950s without changing its charter. But Plan E with PR had been the efficient means for making changes in Cambridge. PR short-circuited some customary political machinations, and Council–Manager government reduced the likelihood of large-scale corruption. It helped, too, that the Depression wound down and that war put new demands on Cambridge industry. The war was probably helpful, as well, in deflecting energies from local politics to graver issues.

The Second World War healed some of the wounds which the Plan E campaign had opened. Some of the ethnic myths expired as young men of all backgrounds went to war against Nazi Germany and Japan. Hitler made anti-Semitism unthinkable. Nearly 15,000 Cambridge men and women were in uniform; 401 died. Cambridge took pride in the crucial roles which Harvard and M.I.T. scientists played in the war effort. World War II marked the real inception of the intellectual shuttle between Washington and Cambridge which is still in service. M.I.T.'s wizard Vannevar Bush served Washington as director of the Office of Scientific Research and Development. Harvard's president, James Bryant Conant, who had been with the chemical warfare service in World War I, became chairman of the National Defense Research Committee and, in that office, took an important part in organizing the research programs which led to the development of the atomic bomb. M.I.T. operated more as a national defense laboratory than as a university—but academic life went on. M.I.T. scientists conducted research on such subjects as radioactive materials, radar, aeronautics, and high voltage. Cambridge residents passing the universities during the war had heard about the top-secret war work being done inside, and spoke in respectful tones. Even the most vigorous critics, including some of those who had charged "Harvard communist plot" during the Plan E campaign, were impressed.

When the war ended in 1945, the mood in Cambridge was upbeat. People were at once relieved by the end of the fighting and pleased with the performance of the new tenants of City Hall and the descent of the tax rate. There was a public bathing beach at Gerry's Landing, and one could find a parking place in Harvard Square. People admitted that Cambridge had problems, but problems were meant to be solved. In 1946 Cambridge observed its 100th anniversary as a city. Cambridge is big on historical birthdays. There was an historical pageant in the Harvard Stadium and a mammoth parade of veterans, school children, city employees, and civic organizations. Harvard and M.I.T. invited everyone for Open House. City notables planted a scion of the "Washington Elm" on the Common, the ailing original having been removed from the intersection of Garden and Mason Streets in 1923.

Cambridge changed more dramatically after the war than one would suppose from glancing at its statistics. As early as 1930 the city had become nearly saturated in terms of population and building. The population figures staged a comeback during the immediate postwar years, reached 120,740 in 1950, and then slid back. In losing residents during the fifties and sixties, Cambridge behaved more like a central city than a suburb—and indeed crowded Cambridge *is* more like a central city, much closer to the heart of Boston than many Boston neighborhoods. The housing subsidies which the federal government distributed after the war encouraged home building in the suburbs rather than the cities. Cambridge housing was miserable. A 1941-43 Works Progress Administration survey of the city's most crowded districts, where 60 percent of the inhabitants lived, disclosed that 86 percent of those people lived in "substandard" conditions—a bureaucratic designation incorporating a wide range of deficiencies from structural defects to absence of plumbing or heating. With the exception of two federally subsidized low-cost housing projects (New Towne Court, 1937, and Washington Elms, 1941), there had been no efforts to improve housing standards. People streamed to the suburbs as government loans and the automobile put the single-family house out of town in reach of the family which used to rent part of a house in Cambridge. Returning veterans found a shortage of desirable housing.

The outflux of population which Cambridge experienced was the rule in manufacturing cities up and down the northeastern seaboard. New York, Philadelphia, Baltimore, Newark, and Boston all lost residents during the fifties as people moved into suburban developments. Industry moved out too, seeking locations in the South and Southwest where taxes were lower and labor cheaper.

Such losses would have left even larger holes in Cambridge's fabric had they not been patched by the birth of new industries such as electronics, engineering, and research and development. Sophisticated, technically oriented firms were drawn to Cambridge—or created there—by the presence of M.I.T. and Harvard and by federal defense contracts. The 1950s brought, among others, Arthur D. Little, the Badger Company, the Electronic Corporation of America, and the Polaroid Company, whose founder, Edwin H. Land, is one of Harvard's most illustrious dropouts. He made his initial discoveries in the field of polarized light and developed a plastic Polaroid film while still a Harvard student; he left school to open a laboratory in Boston. Research and development firms supplanted the brickworks in north and west Cambridge; among the new "think tanks" were Arthur D. Little, Abt Associates, and Bolt, Beranek and Newman.

Professors delighted in consulting jobs which supplemented their academic salaries. One M.I.T. professor who profited handsomely from his private business endeavors was embarrassed at being caught stepping from his Rolls Royce in the Institute's parking lot. He grinned weakly and explained to a less fortunate colleague that his wife had taken the family car that morning and stranded him with the Rolls.

Government contracts also contributed to university expansion during the fifties. For example, the Atomic Energy Commission paid twelve million dollars to build the Cambridge Electron Accelerator, run jointly by Harvard and M.I.T. President Nathan Pusey of Harvard and Chancellor Julius Stratton of M.I.T. broke ground for the installation with a special two-handled shovel in 1957.

Both universities increased their enrollments during the fifties and early sixties, and both of them enlarged their territories and constructed new facilities. Since Harvard and M.I.T. had renowned architectural schools, the postwar buildings reflected current trends in architecture. Two of the most famous interpreters of the "International Style" created buildings in Cambridge in the same year, 1949. Alvar Aalto designed Baker House for M.I.T. (the sensually curved brick building west of Massachusetts Avenue along Memorial Drive), and Walter Gropius of The Architects Collaborative built the severe Harvard Graduate Center. Cambridge's most famous modern architectural object, Le Corbusier's Carpenter Center for the Visual Arts, was built at Harvard in 1961. Few people looked at it dispassionately; they either loved it or loathed it.

The Cambridge collection of contemporary architecture is outstanding. It includes just about everything except a Frank

Lloyd Wright. Some people tour the city just to look at modern buildings. Some of them are very good; others are very bad; most are mediocre. Professional opinions diverge wildly, but this is not surprising since the only building which all architects admit to admiring is the Parthenon.

Cambridge's modern structures are by no means the city's first architectural break with the past—Cambridge, particularly Harvard, is a regular museum of the architectural styles of the centuries—but the present break is one of the most startling. The materials of the past—wood, brick, and stone—have yielded to concrete, steel, and glass. Rising property values dictated the economic wisdom of high-rise construction, for business and residences. Most people responded to modern architecture with about as much enthusiasm as they listened to twelve-tone chamber music. The average Cantabrigian viewed the unfamiliar shapes with alarm. In the late 1970s some people still hated the modern buildings and wished

Cambridge has always loved a parade. On June 3, 1896, Cambridge celebrated its 50th birthday as a city with a mammoth procession. Here, passing through flag-draped Harvard Square, is a carriage bearing the Governor, the Mayor, President Eliot of Harvard, and Henry O. Houghton, the publisher. Camera points eastward along Massachusetts Avenue.

Cambridge still loves a parade. Here are two scenes from the big one that moved from Lechmere Square to the Cambridge Common on July 4, 1976, the 200th birthday of the Declaration of Independence. At top, Cambridge veterans swing from Cambridge Street onto Prospect Street and march towards Central Square. In the other picture a Portuguese group, Romarias de Portugal, based in East Cambridge, passes through Harvard Square. Cambridge has become one of the principal centers of Portuguese population in the United States.

A very modern Cambridge scene. On Brattle Street near Harvard Square a resident looks into a bookstore window which reflects the glass-and-concrete Design Research store across the street.

that Cambridge architecture would revert to an earlier style. But many have become comfortable with the contemporary buildings, have learned to appreciate their good points, and enjoy showing them to visitors.

Postwar Cambridge was a serene place through the fifties and into the sixties. These were the Eisenhower years, when people still believed in authority. It was an age of innocence, a time when Cantabrigians were not cynical. Cambridge made little out of the Korean War. Young men went off to fight, but they went without the conviction or the clarity of purpose which had accompanied them to previous wars. In November 1953 Senator Joseph McCarthy called Harvard "a smelly mess" where students were "open to indoctrination by communist professors." President Pusey responded with cool, intellectual fury and disdained to fight on McCarthy's level.

The biggest disturbance in town came on a balmy May night in 1952. The *Harvard Crimson* was running Pogo for President that year and invited Walt Kelly, the comic strip's creator, to Cambridge. About 1,600 students jammed Harvard Square, waiting for his appearance. The air was warm and things got out of hand as the students started interfering with the electric trolley cars which then ran through the Square. Cambridge police came in and broke up the crowd. There were a few bruises, also some harsh words in the *Crimson*, but no lasting sense of outrage.

For Harvard students, life in Cambridge was just as it had been for three centuries. So J. Anthony Lukas, Harvard '55, once *Crimson* editor and later *New York Times* journalist, remembered that, in his undergraduate days, "Cambridge existed only as a gracious background for Harvard: the fine old colonial houses on Brattle Street, the grassy glories of Longfellow Park, the banks of the Charles. If Harvard needed to expand, it seemed only natural to me that Cambridge should make room as it always had . . ." Lukas as a student had probably never been to East Cambridge. Quite possibly he had never even *heard* of it.

10

Bad News, Good News

The sixties: Students, who had not paid much attention to national affairs since the Second World War, became political activists. Young men and women from Harvard and M.I.T. gravitated south to Mississippi and Alabama and joined efforts to secure the constitutional rights of black Americans. (The students had not yet noticed that social injustices existed in northern states, even on the north bank of the Charles River where they played Frisbee.) President Kennedy, Harvard '40, was assassinated in Dallas. Americans learned disturbing facts about a war in Vietnam, in part from the journalist David Halberstam, Harvard '55. Martin Luther King (who had been a graduate student at Boston University) was assassinated. Robert Kennedy, Harvard '48, was assassinated.

These events touched all Americans, but few cities were as traumatized by them as Cambridge, for Cambridge had an abnormally large population of young people. The children who had been born in the late 1940s—the "war babies"—reached college age in the mid-1960s. Demographic charts bulged where they recorded the 15-24 age group, and the Cambridge bulge was more pronounced than the national bulge. The city's population at the middle of the decade was in the vicinity of 100,000. Figures for the universities in 1968 showed over 15,000 at Harvard; 1,200 at Radcliffe (counted separately at the time); 7,300 at M.I.T.; 1,311 at Lesley College (founded 1909); and 137 at the Episcopal Theological School (founded 1867), for a total which rounded off to 25,000. Not all of them lived in Cambridge; Harvard's Business School, Medical School, and School of Public Health, for example, are across the river in Boston. Nevertheless, nearly all the university students identified with Cambridge during their years of attendance. Add to them the Cantabrigians of the same generation who did not go to college but who lived and worked in the city, and the picture emerges of a lopsided population dominated by disenfranchised young people whose lives and futures were threatened by a national policy which they had not made.

Cambridge got involved in the Vietnam war early, much in the same way it had been involved in previous wars. Cambridge men were drafted and went off to fight. By the summer of 1971, nineteen of them were dead. The universities furnished their intellectual notables to Washington, among them McGeorge Bundy of Harvard and Walt Rostow of M.I.T. An obscure man named Daniel Ellsberg (Harvard '52), with ties to both universities, assisted the Pentagon in strategic planning.

Large-scale student resistance to the war dated from 1965. Cambridge became the northeastern center for anti-war activities. Offices of the national protest organizations set up shop as close to Harvard Square as they could get and still afford to pay the rent. There were Vietnam Veterans Against the War, MASS PAX (Massachusetts Political Action for Peace), the Committee for Concerned Asian Scholars, lawyers ready to defend draft-card burners and others engaged in acts of civil disobedience, and numerous other groups dedicated to ending American military involvement in Vietnam. On top of them came swarms of youthful protestors, drawn spontaneously to Harvard Square as, in a way, the army volunteers had been drawn to Cambridge Common in 1775. Many of these intense young people had dropped out of other colleges; they arrived in Cambridge, shared rooms with friends, and participated in anti-war work. Peace marchers assembled at Cambridge Common, moved down Massachusetts Avenue, picked up the M.I.T. contingent, and crossed the Harvard Bridge into Boston where they were joined by Boston folk for the final stage along Commonwealth Avenue to the Boston Common.

Initially, most Cantabrigians outside

Anti-war demonstration at Harvard in March 1967.

the university community were not sympathetic with long-haired marchers and their cause. Some of those who had fought in other wars considered the demonstrators downright unpatriotic. Others were chronically suspicious of any political activity which originated with the universities. Thus the early demonstrators were overwhelmingly students. But the longer the war dragged on, the larger the marches became and the older the average age of the marchers. The shift in Cambridge sentiment was so subtle that it was perceptible only to the keenest of observers. In 1966 Congressman Thomas P. "Tip" O'Neill—whose business it was to know such things—sniffed the local political winds and wrote a letter to his constituents stating that he would no longer exercise his vote in support of the war. Later he would tell Congress, "My children have awakened me to this war." In fact, O'Neill's announcement was a bit premature so far as the Cambridge portion of his district was concerned. In 1967 the Vietnam question came before Cambridge voters. The Vietnam Neighborhood Association canvassed the city to collect votes against the war while veterans' groups worked diligently on the opposite side. If out-of-town students and eighteen-year-olds had been able to vote, there would have been no contest. But as it was, the Cambridge electorate defeated the petition calling for a "prompt return home" of U.S. forces in Vietnam by a vote of 17,742 to 11,349.

In 1968 Harvard surrendered Henry Kissinger to Richard Nixon. On the other hand, prominent faculty members from both universities spoke out strongly against Washington policies. By 1969 the anti-war mood in Cambridge was sufficiently strong to move the City Council to pass a resolution asking the president to end the war.

Things began to get ugly that year. In April student radicals seized University Hall in Harvard Yard. When Cambridge police, acting upon the request of university officers, attempted to eject the trespassers, the scene turned bloody and violent. M.I.T. students staged sympathy demonstrations, and the atmosphere in both universities grew tense. Thus it remained for well over a year while there was considerable political debate and not a great deal of education in the sense that President Nathan Pusey conceived of education.

On April 15, 1970—almost precisely one year after the incident in Harvard Yard—violence spilled over onto Cambridge streets. That night, after a day of peaceful demonstrations on Cambridge Common and Boston Common against American intervention in Cambodia, an estimated 2,000 people rioted in Harvard Square. Though a number of them were neither residents nor students in Cambridge, they had congregated in the Square, and that is where their rage erupted. They shouted against "imperialists," "fascists," and the Cambridge City Council—for, in their frustration, all governments, institutions, and big businesses seemed to them evil conspirators. But the prime cause of their discontent was undoubtedly the war in Southeast Asia. They smashed windows in banks and shops. Bystanders, some of whom had marched with them earlier in the day, and a few demonstrators and Cambridge policemen got injured before the crowd was dispersed.

Bigger cities could treat such demonstrations more routinely. The student rebellion at Columbia University may have made more waves in Cambridge than it did in the City of New York. But Cambridge, like Berkeley, California, was a student-dominated city. Many who knew and loved Cambridge were distressed. Peaceful protest was an honorable tradition. Random, uncontrolled violence was not. The "trashing" of Harvard Square had been the most violent interlude in Cambridge since 1778 when enraged patriots ransacked Christ Church after a high-class funeral for a British prisoner-of-war who had been accidentally shot by an American sentry.

Many Cantabrigians feared that strong counter-measures by the City Council and Police Department might polarize attitudes within the city and stimulate further disorders. But the municipal authorities behaved with thoughtful moderation and the anti-war organizations worked among themselves to prevent further outbreaks which, they recognized, only hurt their

SDS flag flies from University Hall at Harvard in April 1969. The initials stand for Students for a Democratic Society. The seized building itself, which sits in the center of Harvard Yard, is not visible in the picture. In left background is Widener Library and at right is Weld Hall.

In the spring of 1970 the violence in Harvard Square was not confined to one night. This rock thrower was photographed on May 4 of that year.

cause. In May 1970 the City Council reaffirmed its anti-war stance, this time with a unanimous resolution criticizing the use of American troops in Cambodia and urging the swift, continued withdrawal of all U.S. forces from Southeast Asia. When the Vietnam question reappeared on the ballot in the November elections, only 3,158 Cantabrigians voted for a military victory as opposed to 11,221 who favored a scheduled withdrawal of American forces and 12,633 who supported immediate exodus. The Nixon administration was slow in meeting such demands, which were by then nationwide, but the excitement (and the war) gradually subsided.

In March 1971 Congress ratified the 26th amendment to the constitution giving 18-year-olds the right to vote. Cambridge began to change its rules to permit students who lived in the city to vote there. Students proved to be a smaller factor in local elections than some people had feared and others had hoped. Such political interest as they showed was about national, not city issues. Many simply failed to register. The "war babies" graduated, the anti-war organizations folded their tents and went home, and the new generation of students hit the books as word went around that jobs were hard to get.

For the student activists of the sixties, the war was the heart of the matter, but they discovered dozens of other situations which offended their sense of justice. On any warm, sunny day a dozen or more people were posted in front of the Harvard Coop in the Square passing out handbills about anything from the legalization of marijuana to Harvard's investment policies. Many people in Cambridge could not eat a grape for at least two years without a twinge of guilt, though the grievance was that of workers in California, not Cambridge. Students demonstrated against racial discrimination, against the universities for any number of reasons (admissions policies, faculty hiring practices, dormitory regulations, government defense contracts, campus R.O.T.C. programs). They discovered Cambridge, especially the poorer neighborhoods, and demanded that the universities take a more affirmative role in civic affairs. The protesters were sometimes poorly informed or made childish demands; nevertheless they challenged assumptions and forced reappraisals. They held nothing sacred—and that included Harvard.

Youth attracted more youth, especially during the summers. Some were runaways, without means of support. Many made the Cambridge Common their bedroom and panhandled in the Square. And in the early 1970s the presence of large numbers of these "street people" put a strain on city services.

Harvard has always been a factor in Cambridge, but in the past its effects on the non-academic parts of the city were subtle, describable in words like "aura" or "atmosphere." The real power always lay elsewhere. In colonial days the clergy ruled Cambridge. After the American Revolution, the power shifted first to developers and subsequently to other businessmen. Irish-Americans gradually displaced them. Then, during the 1950s and 1960s, Harvard and M.I.T. emerged as the most powerful economic forces in the city.

There was little cause for conflict between Cambridge and Harvard until the waning years of the nineteenth century when developable land became scarce. President Eliot heard the first timid sounds of protest and explained them away with elegance. He appears to have been sensitive to the possibility that Harvard had responsibilities in Cambridge. But then we see Lowell fretting over taxes, discouraging M.I.T. from moving into town, and buying more Cambridge land for Harvard. Finally there were two universities growing at full speed while Cambridge population decreased and old industries moved to cheaper locations out of town where they could build efficient one-story and two-story buildings and have adequate parking facilities.

The rapid expansion of Harvard and M.I.T. was a response to the national increase in population of student age and the abundance of funds from private foundations and the federal government. By the mid-sixties there was no question that together, the two universities constituted the most potent economic influence in town. In 1974 the two universities owned 428 of Cambridge's 4,000 acres —approximately half and half. Their properties preside over much of the riverbank between the Longfellow and the Larz Anderson bridges. M.I.T.'s postwar acquisitions and conversions of buildings were characteristic of the economic changes within the city. Examples: The old Kraft Cheese Company building on Albany Street became the Nuclear Engineering Center; a factory that had produced library furniture became an instrumentation laboratory; a candy factory at Main and Ames streets was converted to M.I.T. offices. If Harvard and M.I.T. are considered together they are the single largest employer in town. One fifth of Cambridge's labor force works at one of the two universities in jobs including professors, secretaries, janitors, painters, bookkeepers, policemen, herbarium assistants, librarians, gardeners, and physicians. In 1974 the universities' payroll to Cambridge residents amounted to $37,200,000. The "one fifth" does not include the army of construction laborers who build the dormitories, laboratories, and libraries which the institutions need to carry on their work and on which they spent millions of dollars, particularly during the sixties.

Those are the more apparent items, the easiest to tally on the economic scoreboard. Then there are other levels of economic impact. University students are voracious consumers. They spend vast sums of money in Cambridge on retail merchandise such as beer, books, clothing, restaurant meals, hi-fi equipment, crunchy granola, sporting goods, and drafting materials. In the late 1970s they were even beginning to get more haircuts—a fashion revival that warmed the hearts of Cambridge barbers. (One Harvard Square barber was so finely attuned to prevailing moods that in the 1960s he used to advise Harvard professors how long their sideburns should be in order to have good rapport with student activists.) The universities also attract droves of visitors who contribute further to Cambridge coffers. M.I.T. and Harvard estimated that, in 1974, students and visitors spent $16,000,000 in the city. Meanwhile the universities spent $11,900,000 for goods and services in Cambridge.

At still another level of economic impact are the research-and-development firms which have located in Cambridge to be near the universities. These corporations opened up thousands of job opportunities for white-collar, professional, and technical workers. Moreover, they arrived just in time to come to the rescue of the Cambridge tax base. Edward Crane, who was Cambridge mayor during the early sixties, worked hard and skillfully to convince such firms to establish themselves in the city rather than on lower-cost suburban sites. He enlisted the assistance of James Killian, chairman of the M.I.T. Corporation. M.I.T. acted as co-developer, with Cabot, Cabot & Forbes Company, in the building of a new commercial office and research center called Technology Square, which is one of the biggest taxpayers in the city and which acted as a magnet in attracting other firms.

Many of the employees of the new businesses wanted to live in Cambridge but could not find satisfying quarters in the dilapidated three-family and four-family houses dating back to the turn of the century. The alternatives, the single-family homes near Harvard Square, were too large and expensive. Developers responded to the demand with high-rise, high-rent apartment buildings. Also around this time, students found it increasingly desirable to live off campus. The fact that five or six students were willing to pay lordly prices for a few rooms in an old building inspired some landlords to charge them accordingly. In the ten years between 1960 and 1970 the average rent of a Cambridge apartment increased by nearly 90 percent.

Few Cantabrigians, whether they approved of the architecture or not, denied that the streamlined research and development offices contributed to a more attractive, healthier environment than the old industries. It was hard to be nostalgic about slaughterhouses and soap factories. But blue-collar laborers had trouble finding jobs. It is estimated that in one five-year period, 1967 to 1971 inclusive, Cambridge lost 5,500 manufacturing jobs—almost a quarter of all such jobs in the city. Cambridge also suffered a great disappointment when the federal government canceled its plans to build a huge research complex of the National Aeronautics and Space Administration (NASA) near Kendall Square. Factories had been moved, land cleared, and two buildings constructed before the project was scrapped, leaving a lot of empty renewal land and the problem of getting it developed. And although there was some desperately needed new housing, sky-rocketing rents strained the budgets of middle-income families, the poor, and those who depended on fixed incomes such as social security checks. Civic activists complained that Cambridge improvements came at the expense of those people least able to afford them.

Those segments of the Cambridge community adversely affected by the new trends tended to deposit the blame for their woes on the universities. The rent question was a particularly sore subject with the 75 percent of Cambridge residents who were tenants rather than owners. Town-and-gown relationships grew very strained. M.I.T.'s Killian took the initiative. Observing the crisis in low-cost housing and the red tape in which city agencies became tangled as they tried to use state and federal funds, Killian convinced Pusey to form the Cambridge Corporation. Killian's idea was to create a university-backed agency which could act as a catalyst between those who provided the funds to build low-cost housing and those who expressed the need for it. The Cambridge Corporation succeeded in sponsoring 800 units of new housing and in rehabilitating another 700 units, as well as in stimulating additional rehabilitation efforts. However, the Corporation was weakened when M.I.T. took a separate initiative and built three low-cost developments on its own under the Turnkey Program (these projects were turned back to the city), and when Harvard also began to act independently. The Cambridge Corporation went out of business in 1975. Nevertheless, both through the Cambridge Corporation and independently, the universities were instrumental in getting some housing for the disadvantaged and the elderly.

Education comes first at Harvard and M.I.T. They still are less involved in civic affairs than their most forceful critics would like. But, on the whole, the universities have demonstrated themselves to be far more responsive to Cambridge's civic problems than in the past. Both of them now have special offices of community relations. Both institutions give more in money and services than ever before. M.I.T. is Cambridge's third largest taxpayer (by virtue of owning more *taxable* real estate than Harvard), and Harvard the fourth. They make voluntary in-lieu-of-taxes payments beyond the sums they pay on their taxable properties. In the fiscal year 1974-75 their total payments in lieu of taxes were approximately $800,000. More important, Harvard and M.I.T. have learned to tread more gently and to consult with community groups on development plans which are likely to affect them.

Such negotiations are delicate operations, for much of Cambridge still looks upon the universities with hostility—though probably less than they did at the end of the sixties. Harvard is more vulnerable to attack than M.I.T.; it is bigger, older, richer, and has taken less initiative in Cambridge than M.I.T. Because M.I.T.'s expansion has tended to take place in blighted industrial areas, Harvard has probably disturbed more residents. The universities recognize the inevitability of friction between town and gown and face it stoically. As the most prominent objects in Cambridge, they expect abuse. If their posture is defensive, that is understandable. When a community relations-man snaps impatiently, "Listen, if it weren't for Harvard and M.I.T., Cambridge would be another Somerville or Newark, New Jersey," he takes the wind out of many arguments.

As for Cantabrigians, feelings about the universities run the complete emotional gamut. There are those for whom they can do no wrong, and those for whom they can do nothing right. Yet in the hearts of most Cambridge persons there is a soft spot for Harvard and M.I.T. They would much rather do battle with the universities than with General Motors.

Students have not been the only demonstrators in Cambridge. Residents have done some protesting of their own, sometimes effectively. In 1963, when the Massachusetts Department of Public Works wanted to chop down the handsome sycamores along Memorial Drive to build an underpass at the Larz Anderson Bridge (where the "Great Bridge" had been in the old days), Cantabrigians defended their trees in force, posted "minutemen" to guard them against axes and buzz-saws, and shouted the cry of "Save the sycamores" through the city. In characteristic Cambridge style, Harvard botanists pointed out that the sycamores were not sycamores at all, but specimens of *Platanus acerifolia*, the London plane tree. But the campaign had been launched to the cadence of sycamores, and there it stayed. The sycamores were saved.

The Inner Belt posed a more serious problem, for it threatened people, not trees. This eight-lane highway had first been proposed by the Massachusetts Department of Public Works in 1948 as a means of carrying trucks and other traffic through Boston without going through its core. A section of the highway's path lay in Cambridge. Cambridge arteries had not been designed to digest large volumes of high-speed traffic. Though the proposal had not been implemented, it remained very much in favor with the Department of Public Works. The plan called for a huge thoroughfare to slice through Cambridgeport from south to north, crossing from Boston at the Boston University Bridge, up Brookline Street, and continuing northward to Somerville. It looked impressive on paper and may well have been a traffic manager's dream. But it was a Cambridge resident's nightmare. No system of underpasses, overpasses, and ramps could alter the certainty that the Inner Belt would slash the city into unequal parts, encourage

high-speed traffic, create additional hazards for the already overwrought Cambridge pedestrian, and constitute an eyesore. Much worse: it would shove 4,500 people out of their homes and leave others stranded on the unlovely fringes of the highway. Most of these people had moderate incomes or were downright poor. Some of them had lived in Cambridgeport all their lives.

When the Inner Belt project was revived in earnest during the sixties it was embellished by proposals to provide low-cost housing for those whom the road would displace. The highway was now wrapped in fancy words and designated an "urban renewal package." The people whose houses were at stake were not impressed. Said one, "I wouldn't want low cost housing even if they did build it. The very name 'low cost' indicates to me that it would be crowded with no privacy." A woman expressed her doubts succinctly: "If they took me, who says I'd end up in a better neighborhood? I'd end up worse off." Cambridgeport residents—largely those who owned homes in the highway's tentative path—began to band together to challenge it.

When the state proposed an alternative route along the railroad right-of-way behind M.I.T., the Institute acted swiftly to kill it because it would have cut through their properties and, they said, traffic would have caused vibrations interfering with the sensitive work carried on in M.I.T. laboratories. The state reverted to the earlier proposal. Clergymen, businessmen, and the Cambridge Civic Association (offspring of the citizens' coalition which put together Plan E) supported the Cambridgeport residents. The only Cambridge supporters of the Inner Belt were a few members of the Chamber of Commerce, who saw it as a good trucking route, and the city planning director. Politically the Belt was poison. Cambridge refused to look kindly upon any of the routes which the Department of Public Works proffered. The project had no champions in City Council, and two Cambridge representatives in the State House—Senator Francis X. McCann and Representative John J. Toomey of anti-Plan E fame—fought it fiercely. This was one of those rare causes which brought the city together, and together the city triumphed. The Inner Belt died.

Such cohesiveness as was achieved on the highway issue disintegrated during the squabble over the John F. Kennedy library and museum. This is an intricate tale. It began back in 1965 when the Kennedy family, acting through a special corporation created for this purpose, proposed to locate the Kennedy library at Harvard. A 12-acre site was designated west of Boylston Street and north of Memorial Drive where the huge facilities for repairing and maintaining subway trains and trolleys had existed since 1912. Harvard's Kennedy School of Government was to be on the site too. The Kennedy foundation sponsored an architectural competition, and I. M. Pei was selected to design the whole complex. Pei interviewed the appropriate parties and met with members of the community, whom he charmed. However, his first design raised numerous objections, aesthetic and otherwise; he went back to the drawing boards to work on revisions.

Meanwhile, some people in the vicinity of Harvard Square had doubts about the whole idea. They raised objections concerning the appropriateness of the design, but their main concern was the likelihood that the Kennedy memorial would attract hordes of tourists. This would generate further traffic and parking problems in Harvard Square and might produce a honky-tonk atmosphere which could spill over into residential areas. The project

The view from a Cambridge balcony. The time is July 1976. Camera is at 1010 Memorial Drive, aimed approximately east. The drive itself is in the foreground, and across the river on the Boston side is Soldiers Field Road. The bridge is the Larz Anderson. Beyond it the two tallest objects on the horizon are the Prudential Tower and, farther left, the John Hancock Building, both in Boston's Back Bay. In the distance, just left of center, are the skyscrapers of downtown Boston.

stalled while an environmental impact study was made and lawsuits were threatened. The Kennedy family indicated a willingness to split up the memorial and put the library and museum on separate sites. Alternative locations were proposed in the metropolitan Boston area. Harvard declared for the library but remained quiet about the museum. Meanwhile, down in Texas, the Lyndon B. Johnson presidential library had been completed.

Ostensibly a Harvard committee was in the process of examining the environmental impact study when the Kennedys pulled the project out of Cambridge altogether in November 1975. The entire Kennedy memorial went to the Boston campus of the University of Massachusetts. Reactions to the withdrawal were mixed. The opponents were delighted, though some of them would have liked to see the library in Cambridge. Harvard was disappointed to lose the library. But the people who know most about Cambridge say that if there had ever been a referendum on the question, Cambridge citizens would have voted overwhelmingly in favor of both the museum and the library, as did a majority of the City Council.

A journalist recently asked Daniel Patrick Moynihan (Harvard professor and Cambridge resident when he was not in Washington, India, the United Nations, or taking part in national politics) if he preferred any historical era. "I wouldn't want to have lived any time before novocaine," Moynihan replied. "Anyone who longs for the good old days doesn't know very much about them."

Though far from perfect, contemporary Cambridge is a healthier place than ever before. Fatal epidemic disease has long been banished. There are public sewers, and the garbage gets collected. The streets are paved so that people do not have to wade through mud in wet weather. Houses have central heating and plumbing. In the good old days, it did not matter how rich a man was: Spencer Phips used a privy, smelled the garbage, soiled his boots, shivered even at home in cold weather, and was susceptible to smallpox like the stable boy who curried his horses. The Charles River of the 1970s was not swimmable, but it smelled better than it had. Cambridge air was not pure, but compared to the pollution in coal-burning days, it was not so bad. Furthermore, there was an abundance of novocaine, whereas, a century before, Dr. Charles Bullock excavated decayed teeth using a revolutionary but not totally effective painkiller called gas in his offices at 569 Massachusetts Avenue.

Education in the 1970s left much to be desired, and there were many education-conscious parents in Cambridge who lived modestly so that they could send their children to one of the city's superior private schools. Public schools had suffered a decline during the fifties—when so many public systems throughout the country had trouble accommodating the "war baby" population—followed by a school building program after John Curry, a former schoolmaster, became City Manager (1952-1966). During the sixties, however, there were racial disturbances in some schools. Still, the Cambridge public schools were certainly available to more people than they were in colonial days when only boys received an education, and better than they were during most of the nineteenth century when they were overcrowded and understaffed.

Adult Cantabrigians have the right to vote, whether they own property or not, and to bring their complaints before the City Council.

Cambridge has poor people, but the conditions of their poverty would stir the nineteenth-century immigrants to envy. There are no more squatter settlements on marshlands and no squalid ghettos. Such comparisons are of small comfort to those who are poor today, however.

Commercial strips, such as the one along the Alewife Brook Parkway between Fresh Pond and Route 2, offend the eye. But as Cambridge no longer permits random development, there is hope of reversing some of the old abuses. In the mid-seventies there was a marked trend toward "down zoning," that is, lowering the heights and densities allowed for new buildings. There are more green spaces and gardens, public and private, handkerchief-size and larger, than anyone would expect in a city so densely populated. Brattle Street, where Tories once strutted in red-heeled shoes and three-cornered hats, is still breathtakingly beautiful.

Problems persist. Some of them, like the tax rate, seem immortal. In 1967 the tax rate was $82.50 per $1,000; by 1975 it hit $185.30. The reasons behind the rise are not mysterious. During the same period, the amount which Cambridge had to raise through taxation in order to discharge its services rose by 149 percent while the tax base increased by only 11 percent.

The record on rents is better. Not surprisingly, the rent control issue drew more people to the voting booths than the Vietnam referenda. Rent control came to Cambridge in March 1970. Since that date, no individual rent increases have been permitted which would allow a landlord more than his 1967 profit margin. (A few categories of housing are exempt from controls, the most important being two-family or three-family houses lived in by the owner.) In addition, the city now has more than 2,800 new or rehabilitated units of housing for the elderly and people with low incomes. Nevertheless, Cambridge's disadvantaged citizens are still under pressure, and the tenants' movement remains active. Housing remains a serious problem, and the character of the city in future years depends a great deal on how its authorities tackle that problem.

Cambridge people, like most people in America, complain about their city government. Of the twenty-five or so cities that experimented with PR, only Cambridge has stuck with it. In the 1970s even some of the old reformers have had second thoughts. One former champion of Plan E wonders whether it is justifiable to operate under a voting system which many voters do not comprehend. Businessmen and political leaders have been critical of PR, saying it accentuates the fragmentation within the city. Gardner Bradlee, president of the Cambridge Trust Company, remarked, "There are 25 different points of view on each issue, and they all want to be represented. It's very difficult to get a consensus and there is no one today capable of forming a coalition." Bradlee is one of many who regrets the political passing of Ed Crane, who played the power game in Cambridge more imaginatively than any individual in recent history and who, in partnership with City Manager John Curry, got the city moving in the fifties and early sixties.

PR was on the ballot five times from 1952 to 1965, and the voters continued to support it. One reason that the form has survived is that Cambridge has been relatively scandal-free. Such corruption as has been uncovered has been of the nickel-and-dime variety, in contrast, for example, with neighboring Boston. Minority groups now represented on City Council are afraid of losing their voices. Though, as one critic complains, PR enables "a group of 300 citizens to throw their weight around," it also provides small interest groups with defenses against big power. PR gave Cambridge its first Italian mayor and its first woman mayor; and it provides a forum for dialogue among the city's diverse interests. On the more frivolous side, Cambridge folk enjoy being unique. Local elections are amusing. Once the Council has been elected, there is the fun of watching them select a Mayor. This jockeying for position can go on for dozens of ballots until five of the nine Councillors strike a deal and agree to agree. After more than three decades, the electoral process in Cambridge has become almost as traditional and picturesque as Harvard Yard.

Cambridge would not be quite complete without Boston. Cantabrigians rely on the south side of the river for the symphony, the ballet, the opera, the Broadway theater, the Celtics, the Bruins, and the Red Sox. Still, Cambridge has kept its identity intact against all odds. Christopher Rand reported in his book *Cambridge U.S.A.* that a European-born professor told him: "I was brought up partly in Paris—I went to the Sorbonne among other things. I could easily see then why Paris was a great center. All those roads had been planned that way, by all those Louis . . . But Cambridge isn't that way at all. Nobody planned roads leading here that I can see. And yet

Tip O'Neill in his home town. Thomas P. O'Neill, Jr., U.S. Representative from the 8th Congressional District, addresses old friends in June 1976 at their annual reunion at Barry's Corner in North Cambridge. The reunion aroused more than usual interest because O'Neill, the Majority Leader of the House, was expected soon to become Speaker.

Cambridge is a great center, as great, perhaps, as any in the world now. It has a strange magnetism. I can't understand that magnetism, but I still feel it."

Cambridge essences must be savored bit by bit. East Cambridge is still somewhat isolated out on the Point where Thomas Graves once built his lonely house. The homes there now are simple, but residents take pride in them, fix them up, and plant little gardens. Neighbors chat on the sidewalks, and there are some old-timers who remember when they could see the tower on Memorial Hall from the corner of Sciarappa and Cambridge streets. They tell the fable about Abe Cohen who started as a harness maker and converted a ten-dollar investment into Lechmere Sales, one of the biggest discount houses in New England and the only reason why most outsiders ever venture into East Cambridge, unless they have business with the courts. The new Middlesex County Courthouse stands in East Cambridge; there was a sensational cost over-run, but that was a county, not a Cambridge, scandal.

A former editor of the *Cambridge Chronicle* calls North Cambridge the place where "the *real* old Cambridge families live now." For generations this has been the most stable part of the city, its political backbone. Some French Canadian and Irish families have been there for a century or more. This is Tip O'Neill's bailiwick, and he knows the district well. "I have an agreement with John Kenneth Galbraith," he says. "I don't say anything bad about him, and he doesn't endorse me at election time."

Central Square mixes Main Street U.S.A. with more exotic influences which reflect the tastes of students—mostly from M.I.T.—and the variety of the surrounding population. There is a Turkish gift shop, a Spanish-American record shop, and an Indian bazaar. On the Western Avenue side is a little lunch counter where Greek is spoken as often as English. Up on Inman Square the flavor is more Portuguese. Now that Harvard influences have reached that far, one can find *quiche lorraine* as well as Portuguese fisherman's soup. (In terms of food, Julia Child, a resident of Irving Street, has been a big influence.)

And then, of course, there is basic sightseer Cambridge. Harvard Yard is soothing. Harvard's newer buildings are at least exciting, though not acceptable to all tastes. The Cambridge Common and Brattle Street exude tradition, and the imagination peoples the streets with characters out of history books. Lovely, shaded streets of less renown house some of the leading architects, doctors, scientists, lawyers, political figures, writers, and academicians in the world. Cambridge is accustomed to such presences, and does not make a fuss; so Cambridge is still considered a good place to think, provided one has the intellectual wherewithal.

Sooner or later all Cambridge meets at Harvard Square, now as ever the heart of

People in a hurry — the center of Harvard Square in July 1976. Here are two views of the same crossing from opposite directions. ABOVE: Looking west through a tangle of pedestrians and cars toward the Harvard Coop department store (right) and down Brattle Street (left). BELOW: Looking east at the subway kiosk, with Harvard Yard in background.

the city. When visitors first see it the Square does not conform to their expectations. Those who expect a "square" in the classic sense—a place of ceremonial dignity like Trafalgar Square, Red Square, or the more subdued gracious squares of New England villages, are unprepared for a traffic scene from the Keystone Cops, and a square which is not a square at all but more of a triangle leaking out down Massachusetts Avenue and Boylston Street, and spilling over into Brattle Square. A small miracle happens here. Harvard Square lives. It is the most exciting, cosmopolitan, amusing intersection between Montreal and New York. The richness and variety of life obscure the flaws.

Half the world passes before the Harvard Coop during a few sunny hours on a May afternoon. The people are all colors and ages and sizes. They come to shop or eat, and the dozens of little stores and restaurants are there to cater to a wide spectrum of desires. The people browse at the newsstands, they gossip, they lick an ice cream cone, and they watch other people. Sometimes there are street musicians and jugglers for extra entertainment. People pass through on their way from Boston to Arlington, or from Widener Library to Harvard's tennis courts across the river. There is always a crowd; yet Harvard Square is a place where a Bostonian is not surprised to run into an old friend from Lexington, and where Cantabrigians exchange greetings in passing a few times a week. Most of all the Square belongs to the young, who crowd it day and night even when colleges and summer schools are not in session.

Cantabrigians noticed the shortcomings of the Square decades ago, and hardly a year goes by without some new scheme for upgrading the place and solving the circulation problems. As of the mid-1970s, it had not been possible to get any agreement on what should be done. Traffic is still chaotic. Cambridge police used to stand in a booth and yell at pedestrians who disregarded the lights; they gave that up years ago. Some pedestrians wait for the green; most of them dart, dodge, or coolly walk through the oncoming cars. This hair-raising contest between people on foot and people at the wheel (who may be reversed in position the next day) is part of the essence of the Square.

In the center of it all is the subway kiosk crowned by a huge sign advertising 8 minutes to Boston as though at any minute there might be a stampede out of Cambridge. As long as the kiosk remains, somebody ought to change the sign to read "8 minutes *from* Boston."

A Note on Sources

Mention of Cambridge occurs in so many books and magazine articles that it would be cumbersome to itemize all the literature that I consulted. Therefore, I restrict my list to those which I found to be the most useful references.

The Reverend Abiel Holmes wrote the first *History of Cambridge* in 1801; it is a charming account, but there are several gaps. The indispensable work on Cambridge is the *History of Cambridge, Massachusetts, 1630–1877,* by Lucius R. Paige (Boston, 1877). Paige, who was Town Clerk from 1843 to 1846 and City Clerk from 1846 to 1855, had access to all the Cambridge records and quotes extensively from important primary sources. He also supplies a genealogical register and several useful lists. This treasury of undistilled information is, however, tiresome reading. Samuel Atkins Eliot covered a slightly longer period in *A History of Cambridge, Massachusetts (1630–1913)* (Cambridge, 1913) in a much more engaging style. Eliot tells more Harvard history than Paige does. He also includes an interesting final chapter concerning Cambridge's city planning problems in the early twentieth century.

The some forty volumes of the *Proceedings of the Cambridge Historical Society* contain numerous excellent papers on a wide range of topics; two of the papers are specifically referred to in this text, but many others were consulted. The articles collected in *The Cambridge of Eighteen Hundred and Ninety-Six,* edited by Arthur Gilman (Cambridge, 1896), are also of great value. This volume was published in celebration of Cambridge's first fifty years as a city. *An Historic Guide to Cambridge* (Cambridge, 1907), compiled by members of the Hannah Winthrop Chapter of the Daughters of the American Revolution, is an amusing book, full of spicy anecdotes. But beware: there are many errors of fact.

The Cambridge Historical Commission has produced a *Survey of Architectural History in Cambridge* (distributed by The MIT Press). The first volume, on East Cambridge, appeared in 1965; since then there have been volumes on Mid Cambridge, Cambridgeport, and Old Cambridge; the fifth and final volume, on North Cambridge, is in preparation. Thanks to the Commission's work, Cambridge architecture is documented better than that of any other city in the United States. The volumes are generously illustrated and include more historical and topographical information than the title suggests. They also contain extensive bibliographies. Unfortunately, the first four volumes are not indexed, a problem which I am assured will be rectified by a cumulative index.

The Cambridge Book (Cambridge Civic Association, 1966) is a delightfully written, brief look at Cambridge history and civic institutions, with helpful lists and maps.

Those interested in the history of immigration are advised to read *Boston's Immigrants,* by Oscar Handlin (New York: Athenaeum, 1975), which contains information pertinent to Cambridge. Appendices include tables providing ethnic breakdowns of Cambridge population during the nineteenth century, and extensive reference notes which suggest further sources. *Zone of Emergence,* by Robert A. Woods and Albert J. Kennedy (abridged, edited, and prefaced by Sam B. Warner, Jr., Cambridge, MIT Press, 1962), contains chapters on East Cambridge and Cambridgeport. The book consists of sociological surveys by settlement house workers between 1905 and 1914. There are some errors, but the Cambridge chapters are illuminating for their insights into "ethnic" Cambridge at the turn of the century and as a reflection of the social attitudes of the time.

Samuel Eliot Morison's *Three Centuries of Harvard* (Cambridge: Harvard University Press, 1936) is the Bible on Harvard— entertaining and historically impeccable. A revised and enlarged edition is forthcoming. Harvard and M.I.T. archives are rich in university lore.

Cambridge U.S.A., by Christopher Rand (New York: Oxford University Press, 1964), deals with the defense, electronic, and research and development industries in modern Cambridge, and their relations with M.I.T. and Harvard. Rand looks at one aspect of Cambridge during the 1950s and 1960s, and many of his observations are already dated.

Back issues of the *Cambridge Chronicle* provide amusing and informative reading. A special edition published in honor of the United States Bicentennial has much historical matter. Of the Boston newspapers, the *Herald* has usually provided better coverage on Cambridge than any of its competitors.

Finally there are the reminiscences of many individuals who have lived in Cambridge—sometimes just a paragraph or two, sometimes an entire volume. Of these, James Russell Lowell's chapter written in 1854 called "Cambridge Thirty Years Ago" (in *Fireside Travels,* Boston, 1885), provides the most vivid description of the town in the early nineteenth century. The list of people who speak of Cambridge in books, letters, and diaries is as inexhaustible as the list of people who have found Cambridge a fascinating city.

The Cambridge Public Library collects materials on Cambridge in "The Cambridge Room." The library has the only microfilm copy of the *Cambridge Chronicle;* the principal secondary sources including books, pamphlets, and newspaper clippings; also many photographs, letters, and Lucius Paige's notes. The Cambridge collection is not complete, however, and the library staff hopes that those individuals and institutions that possess historical material, including photographs, will take advantage of the opportunity to store them at the Cambridge Public Library where they will receive professional attention and be available to scholars in the future.

Author's Acknowledgments

Walter Muir Whitehill pointed me in the proper direction, as he has done so often before.

Hugh Lyons took me for a tour of East Cambridge in the interest of what he called "the history of *East* Cambridge." Robert Moncreiff guided me through the maze of Cambridge politics and tried to explain PR to me. Joseph Sakey and his staff at the Cambridge Public Library greatly aided my co-worker, Sandra Farrar, in her search for background material and illustrations. Charles William Eliot II steered me to sources I would undoubtedly have overlooked without his assistance.

Among the many persons who shared their reminiscences of Cambridge with me I must mention especially John Tynan and Charles Crowley.

Karen Lewis unlocked the secrets of the Harvard University Archives, even as the materials were being moved into new quarters in the Pusey Library. The staff at M.I.T. was equally accommodating. People in various city departments astonished me with their prompt and willing responses to questions. Charles Sullivan and the members of the Cambridge Historical Commission fulfilled numerous requests for illustrations. Virginia Olson facilitated the preparation of the double-page map of Cambridge in 1976. The Cambridge YMCA, the Boston Athenaeum, the *Boston Globe, Harvard Magazine,* and the *Cambridge Chronicle* also provided photographs. (For complete list of credits see page 129.)

I am especially grateful to Jane Reed, the Director of the Cambridge Bicentennial Corporation, for her assistance and her sense of humor. I appreciated Maryellen Fitzgerald's efficiency and wry observations about Cambridge. Sandra Farrar did research, collected illustrations, and supplied more moral support than she realized. Eliot Spalding, Charles William Eliot II, Christopher Reed, and Robert Moncreiff agreed to review the manuscript and made constructive remarks upon it.

The Cambridge Bicentennial Corporation, which asked me to write this book, also engaged a designer and an editor. It has been a pleasure to work with Daniel J. McCarron, who did the design; with Priscilla McCarron, who did the layout; and with Max Hall, a patient, scrupulous editor who has advised me well.

List of Illustrations

Maps

Cambridge in 1976 .. (precedes Chap. 1)
Street development (four maps) 4, 5
Cambridge environs, 1640 11
Old Cambridge, 1670 15
Tory Row estates, 1774 21
Charles River bridges 39
Cambridge in 1830 46
East Cambridge in 1879 63

Other Illustrations

Technology Square .. (precedes Chap. 1)
Harvard Class Day, 1858 2
Aerial view of Harvard 7
Governor John Winthrop 10
Old Cambridge's parsonage 17
The Rev. East Apthorp 22
Christ Church (exterior) 22
Massachusetts Hall 24
William Brattle 26
"Elmwood" 27
William Dawes Memorial 28
Washington Elm 30
Wadsworth House 30
Fort Washington cannon 31
Christ Church (interior) 33
Elbridge Gerry 35
Longfellow House 37
Cambridgeport scene, 1820s 41
County Courthouse, 1848 44
Cambridge Common 47
Harvard Square, 1830 49
Margaret Fuller 52
Washington Allston 52
St. John's Church 56
Lieutenant Rafferty 58
Harvard railroad station 60
Horse cars, about 1858 61
John P. Squire plant 64
First Baptist Church 66
Tenements on Main Street 66
Bicycle craze 67
Cattle market, N. Cambridge 68
Evolution of Memorial Hall
  (three views) 70, 71
Harvard Square, 1850s 73
Museum of Comparative Zoology 76
Snow on Trowbridge Street 77
Cambridge police, 1915 78
The old YMCA, 1883 81
City Hall 83
Harvard Square, 1885 85
Church Street, 1900 86
Dredging the Charles 88
Harvard Bridge, pre-M.I.T. 88
Upper Charles at low tide 89
Magazine Beach, 1899 89
Charles River basin 91
Bucentaur, M.I.T. barge 91
Harvard Square trolleys 92
Digging the subway 93
Ornate subway kiosk 93
Oarsmen on the river 94
Subway and trolley yards from
  the air, 1929 95
The Immigrant Boy 96
YMCA class for immigrants 98
Recreation in E. Cambridge 98
Counting the votes 102
Central Square, 1930s 104
1896 parade 108
1976 parade (two views) 109
Design Research reflected 110
Anti-war demonstration, 1967 112
University Hall seized, 1969 113
Rock thrower, 1970 114
View from balcony 118
Tip O'Neill in home town 122
People and cars in Harvard Square
  (two views) 123

Illustration Credits

Front cover: Fireworks, © Norman Hurst; Carpenter Center (middle of bottom row), Christopher S. Johnson. Other photographs also appear inside book.

Back cover photograph, Imre Halasz.

Map preceding Chapter 1, Cambridge Department of Community Development (Graphics and Research); adapted for this book by Virginia Olson of that agency.

Photograph preceding Chapter 1, Gorchev & Gorchev, courtesy *Cambridge Chronicle*.

Pages 2, 35, 49, 52 (left), 64, 68, courtesy Boston Athenaeum, copied by Christopher S. Johnson.

4, 5, 11, 15, 39, 41, 44, 46, 61, 63, 66 (bottom), 88 (both pictures), 89 (bottom), Cambridge Historical Commission.

7, Laurence Lowry.

10, Art Commission, Commonwealth of Massachusetts.

17, 30 (top), 60, 66 (top), 73, 76, 77, 85, 86, 89 (top), 92, 95, 108, Harvard University Archives.

21, Daniel J. McCarron and *Harvard Magazine*.

22 (silhouette), courtesy Christ Church.

22 (church), E. Anne Robinson.

24, 31, 109 (top), 110, 118, © 1976, Norman Hurst.

26, anonymous loan to Fogg Art Museum (George M. Cushing, photographer).

27, Judith Parker.

28, 71, Christopher S. Johnson.

30 (bottom), 91 (top), Christopher Reed.

33, Paul Birnbaum.

37, Steven S. T. Lo.

47, 83, *Cambridge Chronicle*.

52 (right), courtesy Museum of Fine Arts, Boston.

56, 58, courtesy Sacred Heart of Jesus Church, East Cambridge.

67, 78, Cambridge Public Library.

70 (left), *Harvard Magazine*.

70 (right), William M. Rittase.

81, 98 (top), Cambridge YMCA, copied by Christopher S. Johnson.

91 (bottom), M.I.T. Historical Collections.

93 (top), from the collection of Daniel R. Cohen.

93 (bottom), 104, © *Boston Globe*.

94, 112, David H. Hunsberger.

96, Charles Henry Currier photograph, Library of Congress.

98 (bottom), Cambridge Recreation Department, copied by Christopher S. Johnson.

102, Olive Pierce.

109 (bottom), 123 (both pictures), Rick Stafford.

113, Mark Silber.

114, Tim Carlson.

122, Robert Schaffel, courtesy *Cambridge Chronicle*.

Index

Aalto, Alvar, 107
Abbott, Eleanor H., 3
Acton, Lord John, 59
Adams, John, 34, 35, 36
Adams, John Quincy, 36
Adams, Samuel, 25
Agassiz, Louis, 72, 80
Agassiz School (public), 79, 80
Agassiz School (private), 80
Alcott, Bronson, 56
Alewife Brook Parkway, 120
Allston, Washington, 52; *illus.*, 52
Andros, Edmund, 19, 20, 29
Appleton, Frances, 43
Appleton, Nathan, 43
Apthorp, East, 23, 32; *illus.*, 22
Arbella, 13
Architectural history, 125
Arlington, Mass., 16, 38, 45
Armenians, mentioned, 96, 97
Athenaeum Press, 65
Atkinson, John B., 105-106

Baldwin, Maria, 79-80
Bartlett, John, 72
Beach, Rev., 83
Beacon Street (Boston), 87
Bedford, Mass., 16
Belcher, Andrew, 17
Billerica, Mass., 16, 20
"Bishop's Palace," 23, 32
Blacks, 59, 79-80, 97-98; mentioned, 67
Blue Anchor Tavern, 17, 25
Boardman, Cato, 29
Bok, Derek C., 27
Bordman, Andrew, 40
Borland, John, 23
Boston: influence on Cambridge, 2, 6, 8, 38, 121; in colonial times, 10; becomes colonial capital, 16; printing in, 16; siege of, 29-32; distance to Cambridge, 40; Irish immigration, 56, 57; builds Back Bay, 73; and M.I.T., 87
Boston Massacre, 25
Boston Porcelain & Glass Co., 43
Boston Tea Party, 26
"Boston Tech," *see* Massachusetts Institute of Technology
Bosworth, Welles, 90
Bowers, Benanuel, 18
Bradish, Ebenezer, 25
Bradlee, Gardner, 121
Bradstreet, Anne, 14
Bradstreet, Simon, 14, 20
Brattle family, 20, 35
Brattle Street, 23; *map*, 21
Brattle, William, 26, 27; *illus.*, 26
Breed's Hill, 29
Breslin, Jimmy, 99
Bridges, map of, 39

Brighton, Mass., 16, 38, 45
Broadway, 40
Brookline Street, 117
Browne & Nichols School, 80
Bucentaur, 90; *illus.*, 91
Bulfinch, Charles, 43, 49
Bullock, Charles, 120
Bundy, McGeorge, 111
Bunker Hill battle, 29-31
Burgoyne, John, 32, 34, 48
Burying Ground, Old, 6, 53; *illus.*, 22
Bush, Vannevar, 100, 106

Cabot, Andrew, 35, 38, 42
Cabot, John, 42
Calvinism, 13
Cambridge, England, 1, 16
Cambridge, Mass.: prehistoric, 9; site selected, 10, 12; in 17th century, 13-18; in 18th century, 19-34; and American Revolution, 26-34; post-revolutionary, 35-44; *1800-1846*, 45-54; *1846-1896*, 55-86; early 20th century, 87-100; immigrants in, 94-99; *1920-1960*, 101-111; reform politics, 101-106; contemporary, 111-121
    Boundaries, 13, 16, 20, 45
    Population, *1775*, 36, 38; *1790*, 6; *1840*, 53; foreign-born, *1880*, 59; *1896*, 55; *1930*, 100; *1940*, 101; *1950*, 107; student, *1960*s, 111
    Tax rate, *1846*, 79; *1896*, 79; *1930*s, 101; *1975*, 121
    Maps, colonial, 11, 15; *1830*, 46; street development, 4-5; *1976*, preceding Chap. 1
    See also Cambridgeport; East Cambridge; North Cambridge; Old Cambridge
Cambridge Athenaeum, 77
Cambridge Bicentennial Corp., vii
Cambridge Chronicle, 67, 75, 126
Cambridge Civic Association, 119, 125
Cambridge Common: in *1775*, 31; distance to Boston, 40; enclosure of, 47; in World War I, 100; mentioned, 1, 115; *illus.*, 47
Cambridge Conservatory of Music, 67
Cambridge Corporation, 116-117
Cambridge Historical Commission, 67, 92, 125
Cambridge Historical Society, 29, 40, 61, 125
Cambridge Humane Society, 77, 82
Cambridge of Eighteen Hundred and Ninety-Six, 86, 125
Cambridge Public Library, 84, 126
Cambridge Recreation Department, activities *illus.*, 98
Cambridge School for Girls, 80

INDEX

Cambridgeport: development of, 2, 40-42, 50-52; fortifications in, 31; in late 19th century, 65-67; population, *1806*, 41; and "Inner Belt," 117-119
Cambridgeport Cycle Club, *illus.*, 67
Cambridgeport Private Grammar School, 80
Canadians, 59, 69
Canal Bridge, 2, 42-43, 53, 87; on map, 39
Caragianes, Felix, 96-97
Carroll, Father Lawrence, 58
Catholics: arrive in Cambridge, 56-59; in Cambridgeport, 65; establish schools, 80; and temperance, 82, 83
Cattle market, 68-69; *illus.*, 68
Central Square: during Revolution, 29; in *1820*s, 51; in *1970*s, 122; *illus.*, 104
Champlain, Samuel de, 9
Charles *I*, 9, 12, 19
Charles *II*, 19
Charles River: dam, 2, 87; naming of, 9; in colonial days, 10, 16; during Revolution, 29; bridges, 38-40; and Cambridgeport development, 40-42; marshes filled, 73-74; in *1970*s, 120; *map* of bridges, 39; *illus.*, 88, 89, 91, 94
Charles River Bridge, 38; on map, 39
Charles River Embankment Company, 74, 87
Charlestown, Mass., 10, 29-31, 38, 57
Chauncy, Charles, 17
Cheeshahteaumuck, Caleb, 17
Child, Julia, 36, 122
Christ Church: built, 23, 24; as revolutionary barracks, 29; ransacked, 32; *illus.*, 22, 33
Church Street, *illus.*, 86
City Hall, 77, 84; *illus.*, 83
Civil War, 58, 80-81
Cohen, Abe, 122
Common, *see* Cambridge Common
Conant, James B., 106
Concord, Mass., 29
Continental Army, 31
Continental Congress, 31
Cook, George R., 75
Cooke, George, 19
Corbusier, Le, 107
Corcoran, John H., 105
Corlett, Elijah, 17, 18
Cotton, John, 14, 16
Craigie, Andrew: and East Cambridge, 13, 42-44, 45, 47; during Revolution, 29; buys Vassall estate, 36; mentioned, 51, 75
Craigie Bridge, *see* Canal Bridge
Craigie, Elizabeth, 36, 43, 50
Crane, Edward A., 8, 105, 116, 121
Cromwell, Oliver, 19
Crowley, Charles, 94, 96
Crowley, Daniel, 94
Crowley, Mary R., 94
Curley, James M., 64, 103
Curry, John, 120, 121

Dana family, 51
Dana, Francis, 38, 40, 42, 52, 75
Dana Hill, 38, 72

Dana, Richard H., 52, 80
Danforth, Elizabeth, 20
Danforth, Samuel, 26-27
Danforth, Thomas, 19, 20
Darwin, Charles, 72
Davenport, Charles, 51
Davenport, Rufus, 40, 42, 51, 75
Dawes, William, 29; memorial, *illus.*, 28
Daye, Stephen, 16
Design Research, *illus.*, 110
d'Estaing, Giscard, 36
d'Estaing, Count Jean, 36
Dickenson, Mrs. E. A., 67
Dickinson, David T., 99
Dix, Dorothea, 53
Dowse, Thomas, 52
Draper Laboratories, *illus.*, preceding Ch. 1
Dudley, Dorothy, vii
Dudley, Thomas, 1, 13, 14, 18
Dunster, Henry, 16, 17, 18
Dunster Street, 18

East Cambridge: development of, 2, 3, 42-44; in 18th century, 9, 10, 20; in *1820*s, 52-53; Irish arrive, 56-57; in late 19th century, 64-65; in *1970*s, 122; *illus.*, 63
Eastman, George, 90
Eaton, Nathaniel, 16
Eliot, Charles W.: on temperance, 83; Harvard president, 84, 87, mentioned, 69, 75
Eliot, Charles (landscape architect), 74
Eliot, Charles W. *II*, 16, 29
Eliot, Rev. John, 12
Eliot, Samuel A., 99, 100, 125
Ellsberg, Daniel, 111
"Elmwood," 35, 36, 38, 48; *illus.*, 27
Emerson, Ralph W., 50
Episcopal Theological School, 111

Fay, Samuel, 42
First Baptist Church, *illus.*, 66
First Church, 18, 56; split, 56; Congregational, *illus.*, 30; Unitarian, *illus.*, 85, 86
Fitchburg Railroad, 60, 68
Fitzpatrick, Bishop J. B., 58
Follen, Charles, 50
Fort Washington, 31; *illus.*, 31
Foster, Bossenger, 42
Foxcroft family, 20
Foxcroft, Francis, 20
Foxcroft, Frank, 82
Franklin, Benjamin, 31-32
French, Daniel C., 69
Fresh Pond, 9, 60
Fresh Pond Hotel, 60
Frozen Truth, 82
Fuller, Buckminster, 92
Fuller, Margaret, 51-52, 80; *illus.*, 52

Gage, Thomas, 26, 27
Galbraith, John K., 122
Gallows Hill, 9, 18
Gardner, Thomas, 31
Garrett, Wendell, 40
Garrison, William L., 18, 80, 81

George *III*, 25, 32
Gerry, Elbridge, 35-36, 42; *illus.*, 35
Gilman, Arthur, 86, 125
Glover, Elizabeth, 16
Gookin, Daniel, 19
Grand Junction Railroad, 59, 60, 61
Graves' Neck, 12, 13
Graves, Thomas, 10, 13
Gray, Asa, 72
Great Bridge, 16, 29, 38; on map, 39
Greeks, 96-97; mentioned, 8, 122
Green, James D., 54, 77
Green, Samuel, 16, 17
Gropius, Walter, 107

Halberstam, David, 111
Hall, Jesse, 64
Hampshire Street, 41
Hancock, John, 38
Handlin, Oscar, 55, 125
Harte, Bret, 73
Harvard: influence on Cambridge, 1-2, 6, 84-85, 115-117; founded, 16; Indian College, 17; first commencement, 18; in 18th century, 23, 24, 27, 29; U.S. presidents graduating from, 36; in 19th century, 38, 49-50, 69; Parkman murder, 72; and Civil War, 81; 19th-century growth, 84-85; and M.I.T., 87; football team, 92; early 20th century, 92, 94; and ethnic groups, 97, 99; in World War *I*, 100; tercentenary, 101; and city politics, 103; in World War *II*, 106; and local industry, 107; modern architecture at, 107; and McCarthyism, 110; demonstrations, 112-113
    Illus.: Class Day, 2; aerial view, 7; Massachusetts Hall, 24; Wadsworth House, 30; Memorial Hall, 70, 71; Museum of Comparative Zoology, 76; river scene, 94; demonstrations, 112, 113
Harvard Branch Railroad, 60; *illus.*, 60
Harvard Bridge, 74; *illus.*, 88; on map, 39
Harvard, John, 16, 24, 69
Harvard Lampoon, 84, 103
Harvard Square: ca. *1750*, 24; in *1830*s, 48; in late 19th century, 72; subway station, 90, 92; demonstrations in, 110, 113; draws anti-war protesters, 111-112, 114; in *1970*s, 124; mentioned, 1, 3; *illus.*, 7, 49, 73, 85, 92, 93, 123
Haugh, Atherton, 13
Heath, William, 32
Henry, Patrick, 25
Hicks, John, 29
Higginson, Thomas W., 48, 52
Hoar, Sherman, 69
Holmes, Rev. Abiel, 38, 45, 56, 77, 125
Holmes, Dr. Oliver Wendell, 48, 51, 58, 80
Holyoke, Edward, 23
Hooker, Thomas, 14, 16, 101
Horse cars, 61-62; *illus.*, 61, 66, 85
Horton, Elizabeth, 18
Houghton, Henry O., 65
Hovey, Ebenezer, 51
Howe, Elias, 51
Howells, William Dean, 72

Hutchinson, Anne, 18
Hutchinson, Thomas, 25, 26

Ice industry, 60
Immigrants, 3, 55-59, 94-99
Indians, 10, 12, 14, 17, 23
Industry: 19th century, 51, 53, 55; early 20th century, 99; in *1950*s, 107-108; ice, 60; meat packing, 64; glass, 53, 64; printing, 16, 65; brick, 69, 109
Inman family, 20
Inman Square, 42, 122
"Inner Belt," 117-119
Ireland, Abraham, 6
Irish, 55-59, 94-96, 99, *and here and there throughout book*
Italians, mentioned, 3, 96, 97

James *II*, 19
Jarves, Deming, 53
Jarvis, Leonard, 40, 42
Jefferson, Thomas, 41
Jenner, Edward, 50
Jennison, Goodman, 18
Jews, 97; mentioned, 59, 96
Johnson, Chandler W., 102
Johnson, Lewis J., 102
Johnson, Seth, 42

Kelly, Walt, 110
Kendall, Joshua, 80
Kendall Square, 40, 116
Kennedy, Albert, 67, 125
Kennedy, John F., 36, 99, 111; memorial, 1, 92, 119-120
Kennedy, Robert F., 111
Killian, James, 116
King, Martin Luther, 111
Kirkland, John T., 50
Kissinger, Henry, 112
Knox, Henry, 32

Lafayette Square, *illus.*, 41, 61
Land, Edwin H., 107
Landis, James W., 102, 103
Langdon, Samuel, 31
Laud, William, 12, 13, 19
Lawrence Scientific School, 69, 72
Lechmere family, 20
Lechmere Point Corporation, 43, 45
Lechmere, Richard, 13
Lechmere's Point: after Revolution, 35; and bridges, 38; development of, 42-44; mentioned, 13, 23; *see also* East Cambridge
Lee, Joseph, 26-27, 35
Lesley College, 111
Leverett, John, 20
Lexington, Mass., 16, 20, 29
Libbey, Edward, 64
Longfellow Bridge, 2, 38, 90
Longfellow, Frances Appleton, 43
Longfellow, Henry W., 3, 43, 50, 58, 72
Longfellow House, 43, 50; *illus.*, 37
Longfellow School, 102
Lowell, A. Lawrence, 90, 92
Lowell, Charles, 36

INDEX

Lowell, James Russell, 126; birth, 36; quoted, 40, 48, 50, 75; and Civil War, 80-81; mentioned, 52, 58
Lukas, J. Anthony, 110
Luxford, James, 18
Lyons, John L., 103-105

Maclaurin, Richard C., 87-88
Magazine Beach, *illus.*, 89
Main Street, 41, 61; *illus.*, 66
Makepeace, Royal, 40, 42, 51, 75
Manetas, Peter, 8
Marcy, William, 29
Massachusetts: early explorers in, 9-10; Indians, 10; colony charter annulled, 26; constitution, 34
Massachusetts Avenue, 41, 51
Massachusetts Bay Company, 13, 19
Massachusetts Hall, *illus.*, 24
Massachusetts Institute of Technology: moves to Cambridge, 6, 87-90; payments to city, 94; in World War *I*, 100; in World War *II*, 106; and local industry, 107; modern architecture at, 107; demonstrations, 112; and city, 115-117; and Inner Belt, 119; *illus.*, 88, 91
Massachusetts, University of, 120
Mather, Cotton, 12, 20
Mather, Increase, 20
McCann, Francis X., 119
McCarthy, Joseph, 110
McNamee, John H. H., 99
Meeting house, 18, 24, 47
Memorial Drive, 87, 92, 117
Memorial Hall, 69; *illus.*, 70, 71
Middlesex County, 18; courthouse, 43, 45-47, 53, 122; *illus.*, 44
Mile Stone, Old, 6
M.I.T., *see* Massachusetts Institute of Technology
Morgan, Clement, 97
Morison, Samuel E., 100, 125-126
Morse, Royal, 57
Mount Auburn Cemetery, 53
Mount Auburn Street, 42-43; *illus.*, 89
Moynihan, Daniel P., 120
Museum of Comparative Zoology, 72; *illus.*, 76
Mystic Pond, 12

Navigation Acts, 19
New England Glass Company, 53, 64
Newton, Mass., 16, 20
Newtowne, 12; *see* Cambridge
New Towne Court, 107
Nixon, Richard M., 112
"No-License," 82-83
North Cambridge, 3, 67-69, 122; *illus.*, 68
Norton, Charles E., 75

Old Cambridge: in 19th century, 48-50, 69-73; petitions to withdraw, 54, 57; *also mentioned here and there*
Oliver, Thomas, 26, 27
Olmsted, Frederick L., 43, 74
O'Neill, Thomas P., Jr., 99, 112, 122; *illus.*, 122
O'Neill, Thomas P., Sr., 99

Paige, Lucius, 42, 59, 125, 126
"Pallysadoe," 14, 17; on map, 11
Palmer, Foster M., 61
Parades, *illus.*, 108, 109
Parker, Samuel, 64
Parkman, George, 72
Parsonage, *illus.*, 15, 17
Pei, I. M., 119
Phips, David, 26, 27
Phips family, 20
Phips, Spencer, 20, 23, 120
Plymouth Plantation, 13
Poles, 97; mentioned, 3, 96
Police, 77-78; *illus.*, 78
Population, *see* Cambridge
Porter Square, 68, 69
Porter's Tavern, 68, 82
Portuguese, 59; *illus.*, 109; mentioned, 1, 3, 96, 97, 122
Pratt, Abraham, 16
Printing, 16, 65
Proportional Representation, vii, 101-106, 121
Puritans, 12, 13, 18
Pusey, Nathan, 107, 110, 113, 116
Putnam Hill, 57
Putnam, Israel, 9, 29

Quakers, 18
Quincy, Josiah, 50

Radcliffe College, 69
Rafferty, John H., *illus.*, 58
Railways, 59-62
Rand, Christopher, 126
Randolph, Edward, 19-20
Rent control, 121
Revere, Paul, 29
Richardson, James P., 81
Richardson, Moses, 29, 81
Riedesel, Baron von, 32
Riedesel, Baroness von, 32, 34
Rindge, Frederick, 83-84
Rindge Technical High School, 84
Riverside Press, 31, 65
River Street Bridge, 51; on map, 39
"Road to Watertown," 23
Roosevelt, Franklin D., 36, 102
Roosevelt, Theodore, 36
Rostow, Walt, 111
Roxbury, 10, 12
Russell, Charles, 58
Russell, Jason, 29
Russell, Philemon, 68
Russell, William, 84

St. John's Church, 57; *illus.*, 56
St. John's Literary Institute, 58, 81
St. Mary's Church, 65
St. Mary's of the Annunciation, 80
Salem, Mass., 10, 26
Sargent, Gilman, 68
Schools: colonial, 18; 19th century, 79-80; in *1970*s, 120
Scott, John, 6
Scully, Thomas, 83
Sewall, Jonathan, 26, 32
Sewall, Samuel, 23

Shady Hill, 72
Shepard, Samuel, 19
Shepard, Thomas, 14, 16, 19
Singer, Isaac, 51
Smith, Al, 103
Smith, John, 9, 13
Somerville, Mass., 26, 69; in *illus.*, 63
Southwick, Daniel H., 57
Squire, John P., 64
Stadium Station, 92
Stamp Act, 25
Stedman, Cato, 29
Story, Joseph, 50, 57
Stratton, Julius, 107
Subway, 90, 92; *illus.*, 93, 95
Sullivan, Michael, 103, 105
Sycamore trees, 117

Tax rates, *see* Cambridge
Technology Square, 116; *illus.*, preceding Chap. 1
Temperance movement, 81-83
Toomey, John J., 103, 119
"Tory Row," 23; *map*, 21
Tracy, Nathaniel, 36
Transportation, 59-62, 90, 92
Trolleys, 62; *illus.*, 64, 92, 93, 95
Trowbridge Street, *illus.*, 77
Tudor, Frederic, 60
Tufts, Peter, 43

University Press, 65

Vassall family, 20
Vassall, John, Jr., 23; house of, 31, 36, 42; *see also* Longfellow House
Vassall, John, Sr., 23
Verrazano, Giovanni da, 9

Vikings, 9
Vietnam war, 111-115
Vose, Robert, 40

Wadsworth House, 31; *illus.*, 30, 93
Ward, Artemas, 29, 31
Washington Elm, 31, 106; *illus.*, 30
Washington Elms (housing), 107
Washington, George, 9, 31-32, 35; mentioned, 36, 72-73
Waterhouse, Benjamin, 50
Waterhouse Street, 50
Watertown, Mass., 10
Webster, John W., 72
West Boston Bridge, 38, 43, 45, 51, 61; on map, 39
Western Avenue Bridge, 51; on map, 39
Whitehill, Walter M, 3
Whitney, Henry M., 74
Whittemore, Cuff, 29
Whittemore, Samuel, 23
William and Mary College, 1
William of Orange, 20
Wilson, Woodrow, 99
Winchester, Mass., 16
Winship, Jason, 29
Winthrop, Gov. John, 1, 10, 13, 14, 16; *illus.*, 10
Winthrop, Prof. John, 25
World War *I*, 99-100
World War *II*, 106
Wyeth, Nathaniel J., 60
Wyman, Jabez, 29

YMCA, 3; *illus.*, 81, 98

Zangwill, Israel, 97